MYTHS & LEGENDS OF
YELLOWSTONE

LEGENDS OF THE WEST SERIES

MYTHS & LEGENDS OF
YELLOWSTONE

THE TRUE STORIES BEHIND
HISTORY'S MYSTERIES

EDNOR THERRIAULT

TWODOT®

GUILFORD, CONNECTICUT
HELENA, MONTANA

A · TWODOT® · BOOK

An imprint of Globe Pequot
An imprint and registered trademark of Rowman & Littlefield

Distributed by NATIONAL BOOK NETWORK

British Library Cataloguing-in-Publication Information available

Library of Congress Cataloging-in-Publication Data available

Names: Therriault, Ednor, author.
Title: Myths and legends of Yellowstone : the true stories behind history's
  mysteries / Ednor Therriault.
Description: Guilford, Connecticut : TwoDot, [2018] | Series: Legends of the
  West series | Includes bibliographical references and index. |
Identifiers: LCCN 2018003406 (print) | LCCN 2018028717 (ebook) | ISBN
  9781493032150 (electronic) | ISBN 9781493032143 (paper : alk. paper)
Subjects: LCSH: Yellowstone National Park—Miscellanea.
Classification: LCC F722 (ebook) | LCC F722 .T485 2018 (print) | DDC
  978.7/52—dc23
LC record available at https://lccn.loc.gov/2018003406

♾™ The paper used in this publication meets the minimum requirements of American National Standard for Information Sciences—Permanence of Paper for Printed Library Materials, ANSI/NISO Z39.48-1992.

Printed in the United States of America

CONTENTS

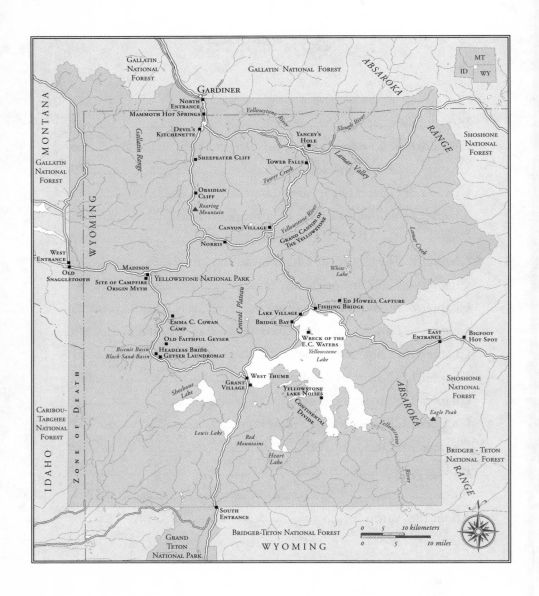

GALLATIN
NATIONAL
FOREST

GALLATIN NATIONAL FOREST

ABSAROKA

MT

ID WY

RANGE

SHOSHONE
NATIONAL
FOREST

GARDINER

NORTH
ENTRANCE

MAMMOTH HOT SPRINGS

Yellowstone River

Gallatin Range

MONTANA

WYOMING

DEVIL'S
KITCHENETTE

YANCEY'S
HOLE

Slough River

SHEEPEATER CLIFF

TOWER FALLS

Lamar Valley

GALLATIN
NATIONAL
FOREST

Tower Creek

OBSIDIAN
CLIFF

▲ *Roaring
Mountain*

Yellowstone River or

CANYON VILLAGE

GRAND CANYON of
THE YELLOWSTONE

NORRIS

Lamar Creek

WEST
ENTRANCE

OLD
SNAGGLETOOTH

MADISON

*White
Lake*

Yellowstone National Park

SITE OF CAMPFIRE
ORIGIN MYTH

Central Plateau

ED HOWELL CAPTURE

FISHING BRIDGE

LAKE VILLAGE

EMMA C. COWAN
CAMP

BRIDGE BAY

EAST
ENTRANCE

BIGFOOT
HOT SPOT

OLD FAITHFUL GEYSER

WRECK OF THE
E.C. WATERS

Biscuit Basin
Black Sand Basin

HEADLESS BRIDE
GEYSER LAUNDROMAT

*Yellowstone
Lake*

ABSAROKA

SHOSHONE
NATIONAL
FOREST

WEST THUMB

*Shoshone
Lake*

GRANT
VILLAGE

YELLOWSTONE
LAKE NOISES

CARIBOU-
TARGHEE
NATIONAL
FOREST

ZONE OF DEATH

CONTINENTAL
DIVIDE

▲ *Eagle Peak*

Yellowstone

Lewis Lake

*Red
Mountains*

BRIDGER - TETON
NATIONAL
FOREST

IDAHO

*Heart
Lake*

RANGE

River

SOUTH
ENTRANCE

0   5   10 kilometers

BRIDGER-TETON NATIONAL FOREST

GRAND
TETON
NATIONAL PARK

WYOMING

0   5   10 miles

N

INTRODUCTION

Yellowstone National Park is a weird place. Its 2.2 million acres are bursting with a sci-fi novel's worth of bizarre natural features, and its stranger-than-fiction landscapes are awe inspiring. Some of it can also be a little unnerving. From the violent, spasmodic eruptions of Fountain Geyser to the medieval, throaty roar of Dragon's Breath Spring, Yellowstone's thermal features alone would be enough to scare off anyone who had never heard of such a thing. That's what we used to think about the Indians who lived in the area—that they'd always avoided this place because they equated the spewing geysers and steaming hot springs with angry gods and spirits. This, as we now know, is a myth.

Our first national park has many such myths swirling around it, and its history is full of legends—in every sense of the word. Besides the visual treats of things like the travertine terraces of Mammoth Hot Springs and the park's majestic geysers and gorgeous hot pools, Yellowstone's rugged mountains and sweeping valleys provide habitat for such megafauna as elk, bears, wolves, moose, and bison. You can get up close (but not too close, please) to North America's largest mammal in one of the many bison jams that tie up traffic, but did you know that the entire native bison population was once down to a couple dozen animals? The capture of a notorious poacher in 1894 was instrumental in stopping the decline of the bison population before it joined the dodo and the passenger pigeon in history's "where are they now?" files.

One of Yellowstone's nonhuman legends is frozen in time as a striking reminder of a troubling chapter in the park's history, when feeding wild bears was actually encouraged. Old Snaggletooth loved an easy meal and paid the ultimate price for it, but the giant grizzly still stands in West Yellowstone, in all his taxidermied glory, a furry fixture in the park's fascinating story.

Possibly the biggest myths concern Yellowstone's "discovery" and the story of when the plan was hatched to create the world's first national park. The life of John Colter, consummate mountain man and veteran of Lewis and Clark's famous expedition, is the stuff of legend. He was long thought the first person to set foot in Yellowstone, but the reality is that he was beaten to the punch by twelve thousand years or so. The proof is right there in plain sight, two hundred feet high and half a mile long. And then there's the storied campfire conversation where the very idea of setting aside the whole of Yellowstone as a "national park" for the enjoyment of the people was first proposed. It's a wonderful narrative that's slipped into folklore, repeated for a hundred years. Trouble is, it probably never happened.

Any place as spellbinding and unique as Yellowstone National Park is bound to generate its share of myths and legends. Let's explore some of the stories, the people, the animals, and the history—both true and not so much—of America's crown jewel of national parks.

CHAPTER 1

Yellowstone's Campfire Origin Myth

As the campfire crackles and pops, Nathaniel Langford pulls his woolen blanket tighter around his shoulders, tilting his head back to gaze at the splendid Milky Way smeared across the night sky. His butt is going numb on the log where he sits, and he starts planning his exit from the conversation. His bedroll awaits.

"That mighty steam cannon—I simply cannot stop thinking about it," says Henry Washburn, the expedition's leader. "It had the appearance of a giant beehive, with boiling water emerging from it rather than bees." He shakes his head slowly, eyes shining, and takes a nip from a small silver flask. "Fascinating."

The other men laugh softly. They speak in murmurs, as if in a cathedral, their faces glowing in the light of the blazing fire. It is September 19, 1870, and the men of the Washburn-Langford-Doane Expedition have camped at the confluence of the Firehole and Gibbon Rivers. The Madison River, its waters black and silver, slips by just to the west. Dinner of roasted venison and biscuits has been consumed and the camp squared away. They can see their breath in the air; the hard chill of fall has settled in over the last few days. There is snow on the ground. The men are weary, but content. Their exploration of Yellowstone, begun in Helena in the Montana Territory a month ago, is nearing its end.

Lieutenant Gustavus Cheney Doane stares into the fire, absently twisting a six-inch arm of his drooping mustache. "The beehive fountain was indeed a sight to behold. And the colored hot pools—they are every bit as enchanting as I've heard. But I'll tell you what I saw: potential. We need to make a claim on this land. Do you not see it? Folks will be traveling out here to see the geysers, the great waterfalls, the lake, all of it. And we'll have a say about how the land is divvied up."

A discussion ensues as more voices join in, talking over each other. "Get title on those lower falls in the great canyon," says one man. "Wait," counters another, "the geyser basin is more accessible." "We have to pool our claims," says yet another. "It's the only equitable solution."

"No." The single bold syllable halts the frenzied chatter. Cornelius Hedges rises to his feet, yanks on the lapels of his heavy overcoat, and moves his stern gaze from face to face as if preparing to deliver a final argument in a court of law. "No," he repeats, lifting his bearded chin. "You are all wrong. This is bigger than any of us. Bigger than all of us. No one should claim ownership of this magnificent land, nor any part of it. Our country deserves better. Yes, I can see that we have a potential for financial gain here. But I propose that we reject all private ownership of any part of this wonderland. We should see that it is protected, set aside as a park for the future enjoyment and pleasure of all citizens. A *national* park." The rumble and hiss of the campfire is the only sound as the men fall silent and look at each other. Several minutes pass as, one by one, their faces transform to reveal their understanding of this magnanimous suggestion. They begin to nod.

"And," says Hedges, extending a finger toward the heavens, as he has, in fact, done many times in a courtroom while winding up his knockout punch, "I suggest we all work individually toward making it so."

Flush with patriotic pride, the other explorers spring to their feet, doff their floppy hats, and begin to gesture wildly, chattering about creating a "national park," a stunning western playground where the wonders of nature will be protected from development, on display for all to see in perpetuity.

Hedges rocks back and forth, a smug smile splitting his silver beard. *This is the purpose of the expedition*, he thinks, *this very instant of inspiration that will pave the way for millions to witness the incredible sights we've seen. This is my moment.*

The story of that fateful campfire discussion, the night when the idea for Yellowstone National Park was germinated, is one of the park's most beloved legends. Nathaniel Langford, who would go on to become Yellowstone's first superintendent, would eventually publish his diary from the expedition, in which the campfire story was laid out in crisp detail. Like most westward expansion pioneers, the men of the Washburn expedition had seen the Yellowstone area as just another financial opportunity. However, Cornelius Hedges, a Helena lawyer, saw something bigger. He saw the future. A grand national park would enrich so many more than just a few miners and land speculators. His vision that night provided the spark that, less than two years after that campfire conversation took place, would spur Congress to pass the legislation creating the world's first national park. It's a powerful story, so inspiring, so convenient. Maybe just a little too good to be true.

Despite a hundred years of repetition and reverence by Yellowstone promoters and administrators, it's almost certain that the venerable Yellowstone creation campfire story is (to use the parlance of 1870) balderdash.

In the early 1960s, Aubrey Haines, Yellowstone's first official historian, started digging into the elements of the famous story. It just didn't add up. While several members of the Washburn expedition had kept diaries, none mentioned the topic of conversation that took place around the campfire on the evening of September 19, 1870. This discrepancy seems unlikely, considering that this watershed discussion supposedly led to the monumental and altruistic decision to lobby Congress to protect the entire Yellowstone area. But it's usually harder to prove something didn't happen than to prove it did.

When Langford published his diary, thirty-four years after the fact, he acknowledged a few changes from the original. "In reviewing my diary," he wrote, "preparatory to its publication, I have occasionally eliminated an expression that seemed too personal,— a sprinkling of pepper from the caster of my impatience,—and I have here and there added an explanatory annotation or illustration." Other than that, he claimed that the 1905 version was identical to the original. It's impossible to compare the two now. The original diary mysteriously disappeared from the Minnesota Historical Society collection, where it was last housed. We could compare Langford's account of the campfire conversation with those of the other expedition members, many of whom kept diaries of the journey. Oddly, though, only two men bothered to write about that evening's events at all, and neither mentioned any conversation about creating a "national park" (a phrase Langford used repeatedly in his published account).

Cornelius Hedges was the other steadfast champion of the campfire story, and, like Langford, he published his diary decades after the expedition but included the campfire story as an addendum. Although his original diary makes no mention of the conversation on the evening in question, he added the scenario to the published version in 1904. Again, since he and Langford were the only two expedition members to write about it, it's difficult to corroborate the facts. Not all of the men were at the camp that night, some having gone off to search for Truman Everts, who'd gotten separated from the party near Yellowstone Lake. No other diaries mentioned the conversation or any reference to the idea of a national park, even though Langford insisted that the next day it was all anyone could talk about. However, by the time their published diaries came out, the campfire story had already become burnished by time and repetition as a factual event. It was only after some scholars and historians began to poke holes in the story, which seemed so dramatically perfect, that Haines picked up the thread and began to investigate in earnest. It didn't take him long to realize that the two men who initially promoted the story, Langford and Hedges, had plenty to gain from its acceptance.

Nathaniel Pitt Langford left his home in St. Paul, Minnesota, to join the Northern Overland Expedition, which aimed to establish a wagon road from Fort Benton, Montana, to the mining regions of the Salmon River in 1862. He wound up in Grasshopper Creek, which soon became Bannack, the capital of the Montana Territory. That designation soon shifted to Virginia City, where Langford went to serve on the Vigilance Committee, the team that was finally able to shut down Sheriff Henry Plummer and his band of road agents known as the Vigilantes. In 1863–1864 the committee tried and hanged twenty-two members of the Vigilante gang, including Plummer. Afterward, Langford continued his upward mobility, being appointed collector of internal revenue for the Montana Territory in 1864. He was also named the national bank examiner. In the summer of 1870, he signed on with the Washburn expedition into Yellowstone. He had his reasons, and they didn't include sightseeing.

The picture of Langford suggests an ambitious, morally ambiguous hustler who always managed to stay one step ahead of prosecution. Rumors and accusations dogged him as he allegedly used his positions as tax collector and bank examiner to enrich himself and others. The most damning evidence of any illegal activity, however, is a letter he wrote outlining a scheme to bilk some money out of the tax coffers. It was addressed to his business partner, Samuel Hauser, with instructions to burn after reading. For some reason Hauser failed to do so, and the letter now resides in the Minnesota Historical Society collection. Soon after Langford's lofty appointments, he and Hauser (who had arrived in the Montana Territory nearly penniless) were somehow able to amass enough capital to open a First National Bank. Langford was never convicted of a crime—never even brought to trial. But, as Yellowstone historian Lee Whittlesey wrote in his own investigation into Langford's history, "He always seemed to be standing close to the till."

Langford's real fortune, however, wasn't in the dirty sloughs and gold fields of southwest Montana. He thought it lay in Yellowstone. The summer before the Washburn expedition, Langford had visited Jay Cooke, a Philadelphia financier who was looking for funding to back a Northern Pacific Railroad line that would deliver passengers to the Yellowstone area. The buzz was growing. Stories had been filtering back East for decades from mountain men and explorers who described an unbelievable mountain territory full of steaming pools of gaudy colors, geysers shooting boiling water hundreds of feet in the air, and bogs of bubbling mud, like a witch's cauldron, burping and hissing as monstrous buffalo and great herds of giant elk and bighorn sheep roamed the land. Langford was an ambitious man whose vision of exploiting the area for his own financial gain was shared by many, especially the men who ran the Northern Pacific Railroad. He'd already been working on establishing a stage line between Virginia City and Emigrant Gulch, just north of Mammoth Hot Springs, and, with Cooke's help, the Montana operator became an agent of the railroad. He was approved to sell bonds to finance the Northern Pacific's Yellowstone line, which would dovetail nicely with his stage business. He enlisted in the Washburn expedition immediately.

The Northern Pacific wasn't just content to run transportation across the West. In the early days of Yellowstone Park, the powerful railroad company seemed to have a finger in every pie of the park's commercial development. Hotels, stage lines, tours, outfitters—the Northern Pacific wanted it all, and men like Langford knew how to grease the skids when it came to land appropriation, government regulation, and the manipulation of public opinion regarding the same.

Cornelius Hedges, the point man in the campfire story, was originally from New England. After graduating from the Yale and Harvard law schools, he became a lawyer in Massachusetts. He married, moved to Iowa, and practiced law while publishing and editing the *Independence Civilian*. In the early 1860s gold fever swept through the country, and Hedges was not immune to its infection. In April 1864, possibly eager to avoid fighting in the Civil War, he walked 1,200 miles from Independence to Virginia City to work the placer mines. Within a year he moved to Helena to work the Last Chance Gulch, and that's where he would put down his Montana roots. By 1870 he had brought his family out from Connecticut, established a public library in Helena, and started working as an editorial writer for the *Helena Herald*. As more and more stories began to drift in about the wonders of the Yellowstone area, Hedges began a campaign to persuade Wyoming to cede that portion of land to Montana. His sights were being set on Yellowstone. He'd worked his way up the legal ladder to become a judge, but it was his position with the newspaper that would figure heavily into the later promotion of the campfire story.

One of the gaping holes in the campfire tale is that Hedges is credited with being the first to suggest the idea of a national park. That assertion has long since been debunked, as there are at least three instances on record when this notion was proposed by

Reenactment of the legendary 1870 campfire where the idea of a "national park" was allegedly introduced by Cornelius Hedges during the Washburn-Langford-Doane Expedition.

others prior to the Washburn expedition. Washburn himself had heard the suggestion the year before from David E. Folsom after his expedition. The idea surfaced as early as 1865, when Hedges reportedly heard it from Thomas Meagher, acting governor of the Montana Territory. To Hedges's credit, his training as a journalist kept him from claiming outright that he was the first to come up with the idea of a national park. Rather, he took pride in the idea that it was his suggestion that all those present at the campfire work in unison to advance the notion in Congress. Although the other, previous mentions of the idea are on record, it was Hedges's series of descriptive articles in the *Helena Herald* about the 1870 expedition that fired the public's imagination and popularized the idea of establishing a national park.

So the only two men from the expedition who mentioned the fateful conversation did so retroactively when their published diaries came out decades later. Doubt had been cast on the story as early as 1932, when author and historian Louis C. Cramton suggested that the campfire story was too simplistic. In his book, which features the unwieldy title *The Early History of Yellowstone National Park and Its Relation to National Park Policies*, he asserts that the true origin story of Yellowstone was a more complex series of events and ideas spread out over time among many of the key players, including several senators and congressmen. Hard evidence that the campfire conversation itself occurred, he wrote, didn't even exist. In subsequent years other historians continued to question the veracity of the campfire story, but by then the tale had been used as a promotional tool of the

National Park Service (NPS) so extensively that NPS leaders steadfastly defended it, even though it was probably apocryphal.

Beginning with Langford, the campfire story was treated with the reverence normally reserved for occasions such as the delivery of the Ten Commandments or the signing of the Declaration of Independence. A singular event that was so easy to encapsulate on a commemorative plaque or in a brochure was just too irresistible. As a promotional tool, it was pure catnip. Langford's embellished account of the campfire conversation published in 1905 (thirty-five years after it happened) was featured in the F.J. Haynes Company's annual *Haynes Guide*, the popular Yellowstone handbook. Park rangers delighted in regaling visitors with the story about Yellowstone's early pioneers and that magical campfire where their heroic generosity of spirit led to the park's creation. The aforementioned commemorative plaque, emblazoned with a condensed version of the tale, was indeed erected at the site of the increasingly mythic campfire. Yellowstone administrators and employees staunchly defended the story, rejecting any and all claims that it was a fabrication. It was just too perfect, too right. The park deserved such a story. In 1971, just prior to Yellowstone's centennial celebration, former superintendent Lemuel Garrison wrote, "If it didn't happen we would have been well advised to invent it."

Still, historians and other researchers persisted in proving the story's inaccuracy, none as dogged in their mission as Yellowstone's first official historian, Aubrey Haines. And perhaps none would have as heavy a price exacted by the National Park Service for his efforts in digging for the truth.

When Aubrey L. Haines came to work at Yellowstone as a ranger in 1938, his fields of study were forestry and engineering, and he soon gained a deep knowledge of architecture, roadbuilding, and the flora and fauna of the park. Aside from brief stints at Mount Rainier National Park and Big Hole National Battlefield, he worked in Yellowstone until his retirement in 1969. Like most able-bodied young men in the United States, he also served in World War II. Yellowstone, though, was his home and his passion. He was a natural choice for the park's first official historian, a position created in 1960. Haines was a tireless and thorough researcher, driven by his love for Yellowstone and its fascinating history. One key element in the park's history, the campfire creation story, would come to drive a wedge between himself and the Washington faction of the National Park Service.

Haines reviewed mountains of evidence that pointed to the spurious nature of the tale and felt that, as a government agency, the NPS should not be passing off myth as truth. In the late 1950s the park had begun staging an annual pageant that featured a reenactment of the campfire story on the site where it supposedly took place. In 1963 Haines sent a missive to Assistant Superintendent Richard Nelson outlining the historical inaccuracies that riddled the pageant's script, which had been written by a Montana State University speech and art professor in Bozeman. Again, Haines stated that a federal agency "should not engage in dramatics or propaganda, as I see it."

The line was being drawn between those who had an affinity for the campfire story and saw it as a powerful promotional tool for the park and those, like Haines, who would prefer that an entity as venerable and esteemed as the world's first national park not engage in the dissemination of phony accounts of park history. Chief park naturalist John Good expressed his concern with the fictional content of the "cornball production" in a memo to the park superintendent, John McLaughlin: "Frankly, there is no support for the pretty picture of an altruistic mind conjuring up a breathtaking idea by a campfire on the evening of September 19, 1870." Good recommended that the pageant be discontinued.

Park administrators didn't see it that way. "This tradition has become so entrenched," wrote Lemuel Garrison, who served as superintendent during most of the pageant's run, "and it is such a powerful factor in dramatizing and focusing attention on the National Park concept, that we would consider it something of a calamity if it were weakened or destroyed through an overemphasis on fine shadings of historical fact."

Eventually park administrators did pull the plug on the pageant, partly due to the controversy surrounding the campfire story, but also because of the *Waiting for Guffman*–like cheesiness of the production.

As the controversy continued to roil, Aubrey Haines would get an unmistakable message of the National Park Service's stand on the issue when he was abruptly assigned to a post at Big Hole National Battlefield. The park was created to honor the ninety Nez Perce Indians and thirty-one US soldiers who died during an attempted ambush there in 1877. It is one of the most heartbreaking scenes of history in the national park system.

When Haines returned to Yellowstone two years later, he found that the position of park historian had been eliminated.

He was assigned to a geology position, where he worked until his retirement. His standing as the park's eminent historian would not go unrewarded, however, as he was later commissioned to write a comprehensive book on Yellowstone's history. *The Yellowstone Story: A History of Our First National Park* was published in 1977, a full eight years after he'd submitted the manuscript. The delay is widely attributed to official hand-wringing over Haines's objective treatment of the campfire story. The massive tome continues to sell and is considered the definitive book on the park's complex history.

Like most skirmishes over historical accuracy, this one is not a simple black-and-white issue. The gray area includes the point that a campfire conversation probably did take place, and the principal characters of the story were indeed there. Original diaries kept by the expedition members support that contention. But even if Cornelius Hedges did, as claimed, bring up the idea of "setting aside" the Yellowstone area from private development, he was not the first to come up with the idea. And it's also true that, like Langford, Hedges had a professional interest in seeing the incredible natural features they'd just explored roped off as a tourist destination. Far from the altruistic do-gooders these men purported to be, they (like most settlers and explorers of the West in the nineteenth century) were looking for ways to exploit this new territory for financial gain. The early history of Yellowstone National Park is rife with hustlers and operators, opportunists eager to get their slice of the national park pie. Not the least of these forces was the Northern Pacific Railroad, whose own man, Nathaniel Langford, went along on the Washburn expedition mainly to gather information that he could use to extol the virtues of a vacation wonderland. The very nature of these acquisitive pioneers makes the idea that they'd eschew private gain in favor of establishing a publicly owned swath of the West pretty farfetched.

What makes a story a legend? To paraphrase Kris Kristofferson, it's partly truth and partly fiction. All the witnesses to the famous campfire scene are long since dead, and there are no surviving accounts in any written form; yet the story lives on, largely on the strength of people just wanting it to be true. Yellowstone's campfire story is so beloved that it has managed to avoid being wiped from the history books despite piles of undeniable evidence that seemingly proves its artifice. Whatever the motivations and ambitions of those men who huddled around the blazing stack of lodgepole pine logs on that brisk September evening in 1870, the idea of one man standing up to proclaim his vision for a national park has become an enduring symbol of Yellowstone's creation. It's like Santa Claus—even though we know the truth, we prefer to believe the version that makes us happy.

CHAPTER 2

Old Snaggletooth

When you have a positive bear encounter in Yellowstone National Park these days, it means you spotted a big black bear and her cubs a few hundred yards away from your hiking trail in the Hayden Valley. Or maybe you pulled off the road between Norris and Mammoth Hot Springs to use your telephoto lens to snap a few shots of a hump-backed grizzly moving through the trees on a mountainside across the river. But in the early days of Yellowstone, all the way through the 1960s, a bear encounter may have had you face to face with a mooching black bear standing on his hind legs to accept a bologna sandwich you offered through your car window.

My, how times have changed. Those of us old enough to remember Yogi Bear used to spend our Saturday mornings laughing our heads off at the exploits of the cartoon bear and his little side-kick Boo Boo as they got themselves into one pickle after another trying to liberate "pic-a-nic baskets" from visitors at Jellystone Park. Their nemesis, Ranger Smith, was constantly yanking his phillips-head hat down over his ears in frustration over the opportunistic bears and the problems they caused in search of food. The cartoon was based on the practice of feeding bears in Yellowstone Park, an activity that was once treated as a major draw and actually encouraged by the park's administration. Times were different then, and we weren't yet aware of the dangers to both humans and bears posed by this custom. Photos of hold-up bears stopping traffic to beg for handouts enticed visitors from all over the country to come out to Yellowstone and get up close and personal with one of the park's most popular mammals. With all we know today about bear behavior and populations, and the delicate balance of the intertwined habitat of all the park's wildlife, it's mind-blowing to think that this craziness went on for almost one hundred years.

One bear in particular has come to symbolize this bizarre era in Yellowstone's history. Today he welcomes visitors to the Yellowstone Historic Center in West Yellowstone, giant paws outstretched, mouth open as if in mid-roar, exposing a fearsome set of choppers including the lower incisor that juts out at a right angle. It's what gives him his name: Old Snaggletooth. He's the most famous bear in Yellowstone Park, and his story is both curious and tragic.

Bear jam might sound like a tasty—or perhaps weird—treat you can pick up at a Yellowstone gift shop, but it's actually a term used to describe the snarl of traffic that signals a bear sighting near the road. While there are plenty of pullouts and parking lots along Yellowstone's main roads, bears can be notoriously uncooperative, popping out of the woods in the most inconvenient places. Motorists tend to pull over onto narrow shoulders or on a blind curve, or sometimes just stop in the middle of the road and jump out of their vehicles (all prohibited by park rules, by the way), to snap a photo of one of Yellowstone's celebrated bruins. The resulting traffic jams are a danger to other visitors (and not too healthy for the bears, either). During the park's summer peak times, you'll see long lines of vehicles stopped on the roadside, with people pouring out of them to see, well, what the heck everyone else is looking at.

While bears are less frequent subjects of the traffic jams (bison are far less wary of people and tend to wander right onto the road, literally blocking traffic), they're plentiful enough that you'll probably see at least a couple during your visit to the park. You just have to keep your eyes peeled. Up until about 1970, however, it was a lot simpler: you just had to drive to one of Yellowstone's garbage dumps around dusk, and you'd be guaranteed a show put on by our ursine friends when they ambled out of the woods to gorge themselves on the refuse from the park's hotels and restaurants. How did this practice come to be? Well, it began almost as soon as Yellowstone was designated the world's first national park in 1872.

Yellowstone is situated in prime bear habitat. Grizzlies and black bears have been around for thousands of years, and the early explorers, mountain men, and Indian tribes who came through the area encountered them frequently. Several members of the famed Hayden Geological Survey of 1871 even treated bear as game, describing the meat as "delicious." (It's an acquired taste, kind of like a greasy, stringy pot roast.) Soon after the park opened, the Northern Pacific Railroad and a few hardy entrepreneurs began building hotels around the park to host the increasing number of visitors who were taking trains out West to visit what was then known as Wonderland. Hotels attract people, people produce garbage, and garbage brings bears—it's a time-honored equation that folks living in the Mountain West know all too well. Bear attractants like dog food and bird feeders bring bears out of the woods in many urban environments in the Northern Rockies. It's a safety problem for people and—as bears become habituated to human presence—a health issue for the bears.

Early park officials, like Philetus W. Norris, Yellowstone's second superintendent, saw bears as a nuisance and a danger to the park's visitors. (Never mind that it was people encroaching on the bears' turf, not the other way around.) Norris took it upon himself to shoot a few of the beasts, and some accounts suggest that several bears may even have been inadvertently killed by consuming poison-laced animal carcasses that had been laid out to control wolves and other predators.

By 1900 bears had become an unofficial symbol of this spectacular park out West. People couldn't wait to travel the dusty roads of Yellowstone on horseback or in wagons to see Old Snaggletooth's forebears up close and personal. The two sites that drew the most bears were the garbage dumps at the Lake Hotel and the Canyon Hotel, both located near the Hayden Valley, an area popular with bears. (It's still one of the best places in Yellowstone to view them.) As the bears came out of the woods at dusk to congregate at the garbage dumps, an armed, mounted park ranger would stand by as crowds of people gathered to watch the bears paw through the mounds of trash, occasionally engaging in an entertaining fight over some bacon rind or orange peel (the bears, not the tourists).

When the first automobiles were allowed into the park in 1915—over the strenuous objections of at least three park superintendents—bears quickly learned to change their behavior.

Black bears in particular were drawn to the appearance of meals on wheels and began showing up at roadsides, where people would stop their vehicles and throw food. As the bears became accustomed to the new food source, people mistakenly took their habituation as a sign that these were tame animals. Far from it. They were still wild animals, of course, and, while not as ornery as a moose, they were big, powerful, and dangerous. In 1916 Yellowstone recorded its first bear-caused human fatality when sixty-one-year-old Frank Welch was killed near a camp in Sylvan Valley while hauling a load of hay and oats.

Once visitors started feeding bears on the roadside, the reports of bear-caused injuries skyrocketed. The park didn't officially start keeping tabs on the numbers until 1931, but the injuries reported were overwhelmingly non-life-threatening bites and scratches caused by bears reaching for the handouts being offered. Park superintendent Horace Albright suggested that not only were the injuries invited by the foolhardy behavior of the tourists, but perhaps the wounds could even be regarded as a badge of honor, an impressive souvenir to take home from their visit. This suggestion was apparently not widely embraced.

Stories of roadside bear encounters emerged over the next several decades as the hold-up bears became one of Yellowstone's most popular attractions. Between 1931 and 1969, an average of forty-eight bear-inflicted injuries was reported each year, along with more than one hundred incidents of property damage. Yogi wasn't impressed with fine tuck and roll leather upholstery; he wanted that picnic basket on the backseat. One Wyoming writer recalled a tale from his childhood visit to the park when he watched a large black bear crawl through an open door into the backseat of a Volkswagen Beetle. The car's outraged owner then proceeded to kick the bear's rear end. The bear, unable to maneuver in the tight confines of the backseat, exited through the other door while the man who owned the car, perhaps unaware that he'd narrowly escaped a potentially fatal conflict, stood and shook his fist at the retreating animal. There are dozens of tales of such knuckleheaded behavior involving Yellowstone's roadside bears.

Despite constant warnings from park rangers and officials that these were, indeed, dangerous animals, people visiting Yellowstone wanted nothing more than to get within arm's length of a real wild bear. Albright recalled one encounter reported by a female visitor who demanded that the park euthanize a bear that had ripped off her dress in the Canyon parking lot. She'd been there all morning, eventually getting the bear to stand on its hind legs to take food from her hand. When the bear dropped back down to the ground, his front claws apparently snagged the woman's dress, pulling it completely off. The park did not kill the bear.

Park officials had mixed feelings about the practice of bear feeding. On the one hand, it was responsible for a constant stream of injuries to visitors to Yellowstone National Park. On the other hand, it was responsible for a constant stream of visitors to Yellowstone National Park. Rangers couldn't help but get in on the act, posing for photos surrounded by feeding bears or sitting proudly erect on their saddled mounts while overseeing a massive "bear show" at a garbage dump. One dump, near the Hamilton Store at Old Faithful, even featured a large wood sign that read, "Lunch Counter for Bears Only." Wooden bleachers were constructed at the larger dumps to give spectators a measure of comfort while they marveled each evening at the sight of dozens of wild bears pawing through giant mounds of garbage, gorging themselves on scraps just a few yards from the audience. By the mid-twentieth century hundreds of bears had joined the nightly ritual. Black bears would congregate at dusk like retirees swarming the early-bird dinner buffet. Once darkness began to fall, the grizzlies would emerge from the timber to move in on the garbage. The black bears, following ursine hegemony, hightailed it out of there, surrendering the food source to even the smallest of grizzlies. Bears are hardwired with a keen sense of social order, and grizzlies are situated at the top of the heap. A thousand-pound specimen like Old Snaggletooth, even with his blind eye and missing claw, would have no trouble claiming his spot at the dump diner.

By 1930 it was estimated that 250 grizzly bears were frequenting Yellowstone's garbage dumps. Grizzlies, like most bears, are opportunistic omnivores. They'll eat pretty much anything, but the bulk of their natural diet consists of roots, berries, grasses, insects, and other forage. They'll occasionally consume carrion or hunt small mammals and fish. They've also been known, if the situation presents itself, to eat people, though this is extremely rare. Several grizzly maulings occur every year in our national parks, but as hikers and campers arm themselves with knowledge, caution, and bear spray, most victims can survive a grizzly encounter. Still, the idea that "you probably won't get killed" wasn't enough to keep people from gathering around the dumps at night to watch these fearsome predators wander in for some grub.

As the number of visitors to Yellowstone increased each year, the popularity of the park's bears was seized upon by the Union Pacific Railroad, whose advertising and publicity department could be as opportunistic as the bears themselves. One full-color ad from 1950 portrays a family of cartoon bears inside a rustic cabin. The door is thrown open to reveal Old Faithful erupting in the distance, the Old Faithful Inn visible next to it. Papa Bear is pointing at a black-and-white television with the stem of his pipe while Mama Bear, wielding a mop, looks on with a diaper-clad baby bear crawling at her feet. "They're Comin'!" shouts the ad's headline, announcing the upcoming summer season of Yellowstone Park and the expected trainloads of tourists. Walter Oehrle, the artist, became well known for his series of cuddly, anthropomorphized bears, which were featured in Union Pacific ads for decades. Yellowstone-bound rail passengers kicking back in the railroad's sleek Streamliner in the 1930s could enjoy such exotic offerings as buffalo roasts and steaks while perusing menus that featured Oehrle's "Yellowstone Bears" frolicking on the cover. It was the bears they were going to see, and the railroad knew it.

Shortly after World War II, possibly influenced by a fatal bear attack at an Old Faithful camp in 1942, the park began to shut down the "public viewing" dump sites. By now the animals were pretty much habituated to the stream of visitors that continued to feed them at roadway bear jams, and they still frequented the dumps scattered throughout the park. These mostly black hold-up bears, not being known for their respect of boundaries, also left the park to hang out at garbage dumps around Yellowstone's gateway communities. The 1960s arrived, and Yogi was a TV star as he continued to filch pic-a-nic baskets at Jellystone Park while Boo Boo, his cartoon conscience in a bow tie, continued to warn him of ranger danger.

The American black bear is Yellowstone's (and North America's) most common bear. Despite the name, they can be blue-black, brown, or even cinnamon colored. They're designed to live off such natural fare as whitebark pine nuts, grasses, insects, berries, and small mammals. But these Yellowstone critters had become used to a diet supplemented by graham crackers, Oreo cookies, marshmallows, and other junk foods fed to them through the slot at the top of a car window. Hmm, moth or marshmallow? It's not difficult to see why bears weren't going to stop their roadside mooching any time soon. It would be up to the Park Service.

In 1970 the sun began to quickly set on the Yellowstone bears' handout heyday. The park banned the practice of feeding bears and closed down all garbage dumps. All waste would now be trucked from the park to sites a good distance away. Another major arm of the park officials' multi-pronged efforts was the installation of bear-proof garbage cans, the design of which has been perfected over the years to foil even the cleverest of hungry bears.

In West Yellowstone, the park's most popular entrance, Old Snaggletooth had been frequenting the dump just north of town for more than ten years, and his easily recognizable features had made him the most famous bear in the park. He was the subject of magazine articles, books, and thousands of photographs. As park administrators were mobilizing their plan to solve the bear feeding issue once and for all, Old Snaggletooth met his tragic end. On the evening of May 19, 1970, a pair of Idaho men entered the town

Old Snaggletooth was easily identifiable by his missing ear, milky left eye, missing claw on his front left paw, and protruding tooth.

Norman D. Weis, 1965. Yellowstone Historical Collection.

dump, where the bear was at his normal spot, scavenging food, and shot him several times with a small-caliber rifle. Game warden Kenneth "Pinky" Sears lived just across US Highway 191 from the dump and heard the shots. He was able to quickly apprehend the two, who gave no reason for killing the beloved bear. The poachers were taken into custody in West Yellowstone, where they paid bail of $200 each. They left the area, forfeiting their bail. They were later convicted, the forfeited cash being their only punishment.

Old Snaggletooth, mortally wounded, made his way into the woods, where he later died. The bear, who reached eight feet in height on his hind legs, is on display at West Yellowstone's History Center. Thieves have swiped his eponymous tooth several times, not realizing that it's a replica. The real tooth, as well as the bear's actual skull, are on display in a small Plexiglas case.

Old Snaggletooth's death marked a turning point in Yellowstone's bear management approach. No-feed rules were strictly enforced, and, once weaned off human food, bears began to increase their range, moving deeper into the backcountry. In 1983 the park established "bear management areas" where human activity was restricted. Today visitors are warned to give bears at least one hundred yards of leeway and are shown what to do in a grizzly attack (there are still a handful of attacks reported every year). People learn how to secure their food at campsites so as not to attract bears, and hard-sided campers are required in campsites known to be in heavily populated bear territory. As a result of these changes, the number of bear-human conflicts has decreased dramatically. The forty-five injuries per year averaged in the mid-twentieth century had dropped to a single injury per year, on average, by 2000.

Bears in Yellowstone rarely need to be relocated, and populations of both grizzlies and black bears are stable.

On the wall next to Old Snaggletooth is a near-life-size black-and-white photo that captures the fearsome predator in an absurd pose. He holds up one paw, big as a catcher's mitt, as if to ward off the camera. With his cloudy eye and chewed-up ear, he looks like a tough customer, one not to be trifled with. This image might be a little more terrifying if he weren't seated on his butt on a big pile of garbage in the dump, a scrap of detritus poking from his mouth, his legs stretched out before him like a toddler on the kitchen floor playing with pots and pans.

As grizzlies go, Old Snaggletooth isn't the biggest, but he's plenty big. To see his mounted replica up on its hind legs, massive paws clawing the air, and to read his story on the nearby plaque strikes a paradox in one's mind. How could this magnificent crea-ture, who resides at the very top of the food chain, have been subju-gated to the position of garbage dump habitué, content to feed on the leavings of the people who were the very ones to invade its habi-tat? It's a lesson that took us almost a century to learn, and today we still shake our heads in amazement that such outrageous practices were once not just accepted but also encouraged in Yellowstone.

CHAPTER 3

Legend of the Sheepeaters

I magine you're an astronaut, serving on a mission to a distant planet—say, Neptune. Although you've seen photos taken by unmanned spacecraft and studied everything we've learned about the planet since it was first seen through a telescope in 1846, you'll be the first human to get a good look firsthand. You're a pioneer. They'll probably name schools after you. Your landing vehicle settles onto the surface, the airlock whooshes open, and you step through the door to find . . . footprints all over the place.

John Colter wasn't an astronaut, but he may have experienced a similar shock when he traveled into the Yellowstone plateau. He is widely regarded as the first white man to encounter the otherworldly region of the upper Yellowstone River that would become our first national park, but by the time the famous mountain man walked into Yellowstone in the winter of 1807, a tribe of Native Americans had already been calling the area home for hundreds, maybe thousands of years. They were the Tukudeka, or Sheepeaters.

Popular legend suggests that most indigenous peoples were afraid of the boiling fountains and hissing steam vents in the Yellowstone region, believing they were angry gods or evil spirits. While some tribes did steer clear of the area as they migrated through the mountains to the hunting grounds of the plains, it was by no means avoided by all. Archaeological evidence shows that at least two dozen tribes passed through Yellowstone, some even making the forested mountains their territory. The Sheepeaters, a band of the Eastern Shoshone tribe, adapted to the unique topography of Yellowstone with such tenacity, ingenuity, and outright courage that they became legendary as a great, mysterious tribe of the Mountain West. Although the earliest white trappers and hunters to explore Yellowstone sent back reports of an intelligent, friendly people, the Sheepeaters would get a bad rap as Yellowstone National Park came into being in the 1870s. They became known as the shy "little people," and their stature is one of the many mischaracterizations perpetrated by Yellowstone's early promoters, as the idea of "savages" living in the park and crossing paths with visitors might keep some of those well-heeled guests away.

Up until about 1990, the general consensus was that the Sheepeaters moved into the Yellowstone area around the time we got our first glimpse of Neptune. But new archaeological finds and emerging technology gave researchers the means to wipe out those old legends. Thanks to recently uncovered sites such as Mummy Cave, just west of Cody, Wyoming, archaeologists have found evidence that suggests the Sheepeaters were in Yellowstone earlier than was previously thought—three thousand years earlier. And they were far from the cowardly, impoverished dolts described by narrow-minded park proponents of the late 1800s. As you'll see, the Sheepeaters were an advanced people who spent many generations thriving in the harsh conditions of Yellowstone and used the area's resources and game, especially bighorn mountain sheep, to craft everything from powerful bows used for killing prey to some

Tribal members of the Shoshone, the parent tribe of the Tukudeka (or Sheepeaters) of Yellowstone.

WILLIAM HENRY JACKSON, 1871. NPS.GOV.

of the most highly prized items of clothing to be found at trading rendezvous. The Sheepeaters were nomadic, moving quietly and easily between the mountains and forests of Yellowstone and the open plains of Wyoming, leaving behind just enough debris from their lives for us to piece together a picture of a complex, intelligent, and gentle people who lived in harmony with this magical plateau in the Northern Rockies.

"Utterly unfit for warlike contention," wrote Hiram Chittenden, Yellowstone's first historian, of the Sheepeaters. "They were destitute of even savage comforts. They were feeble in mind and diminutive in stature, and are described as a 'timid, harmless race.'" Wyoming historian Charles Coutant attributed their short stature to inbreeding: "They became a timid and inoffensive tribe, marrying among themselves and at last became dwarfed."

Historians seemed to find it insulting that the Sheepeaters were not a war-prone band, mistaking this as cowardice. These mischaracterizations of the Mountain Shoshones were disseminated and accepted as truth. Now recent archaeological finds and oral histories collected from tribal members on the Wind River and other reservations have given us a much more accurate picture of the Sheepeaters, and the stories and legends describing an inferior race of short, grubby natives cowering in the forests of Yellowstone are shown to be utter hogwash.

Not all European-American explorers of the West were so eager to throw the Sheepeaters under the stagecoach. Mountain man Osborne Russell encountered a group of Sheepeaters in 1835 and was struck by the finely tailored buckskin garb sported by the happy and content Indians. He also noted that they were laden with pelts and skins from beavers, elk, deer, and, of course, mountain sheep and were eager to trade. Indeed, it was at later trading rendezvous that the high-quality handiwork of the Sheepeaters began to change the views held by the trappers and explorers who were fanning out into the new territory of the West. The mysterious band of native hunter-gatherers would be popular trade partners through the mid-nineteenth century. But scattered conflicts between Indians and white travelers—most notably the capture of a party of tourists in Yellowstone Park in 1877—would spur the government to pressure Yellowstone's superintendent to control the "savages" who were endangering the park's visitors. By 1882 all tribes were banned from the park, and soon after that most Native Americans were removed from their tribal lands and placed in reservations.

Unflattering stories of the little-known tribe of mountain Indians persisted well into the twentieth century. Books published as recently as 1990 claimed that the Sheepeaters had appeared in Yellowstone in the early 1800s, having moved with the Shoshone and other tribes from Nevada's Great Basin. The Tukudeka ("sheep eaters") spoke an Uto-Aztecan language known as Central Numic. This band of hunter-gatherers moved with the seasons from the forested mountains of Yellowstone eastward to the open plains of Wyoming. Like many Indian tribes, they followed the food. Before the transcontinental railroad brought a flood of gold seekers out West, the bighorn sheep was almost as abundant as the buffalo, and the animals were an excellent resource for the Tukudeka, who hunted them with the help of their dogs. Bighorn sheep, which could get as big as 280 pounds for an adult male, yielded plenty of meat, and their skins were highly prized. Bones, brains, sinew, hide—the Sheepeaters used nearly the whole animal. But it was the magnificent hunting bows they crafted from the large, curled horns that were the hot ticket among traders. These legendary weapons were more powerful and accurate than their wood counterparts and reportedly could put an arrow clear through a sheep. As more information is revealed about this reclusive tribe of mountain people, it becomes more obvious that their sophisticated lifeways were far beyond the primitive existence described by early Yellowstone administrators who wanted them out of the park.

The discovery of Mummy Cave, just east of Yellowstone, was a major find that yielded a wealth of information about the Sheepeaters and their culture. Excavation of the site revealed thirty-eight distinct layers that added up to nine thousand years of use. The vast majority of bones found were those of bighorn sheep. Projectile points were also found that supported the theory of the "Numic Spread"—the movement of indigenous peoples from the Great Basin. Some of these points dated back 3,500 years. These artifacts, combined with the discovery of Shoshone-style pottery shards along the Great Basin–Wyoming route, provide a time frame quite different from the widely accepted claim that Sheepeaters arrived in Yellowstone only two hundred years ago. Archaeologists differ in their conclusions, but it is generally thought that the Sheepeaters moved into the Yellowstone area anywhere from nine hundred to five thousand years ago. Other recent archaeological sites such as Legend Rock, south of Cody, bolster this timeline.

Evidently the Sheepeaters had plenty of time to figure out the Yellowstone plateau and how to benefit from its unique environment.

One aspect peculiar to the Tukudeka is their use of dogs. A Sheepeater family unit might have had a dozen or more people, members of two or three generations, living and traveling together. Typically this extended family would also have had at least one domesticated dog per person. These pooches weren't family pets, however. They earned their keep and were treated as important members of the group, and the Sheepeaters took good care of these valued family members. For instance, dogs were usually fed before the people ate.

Sheepeater dogs served many functions, including hunters, night watchmen, draft animals, and bed warmers. The animals were quite intelligent and trained to work entirely under voice command. On winter nights, when the temperature dropped to below zero, they were brought into the wickiups and shelters and curled up with their people, providing some welcome body heat.

The large canines, which had been bred and domesticated from wolves, were fitted out with travois that carried up to eighty-pound loads. The travois, used by many plains tribes, consisted of two long poles with a buckskin or net suspended between them. The poles came together at the narrow end and were attached to a dog or horse, or sometimes hauled by men. Dogs rarely carried children on a travois, as their tendency to chase the occasional rabbit would have produced disastrous results. Sheepeater dogs also carried rawhide parfleches, envelope-like saddlebags that were stuffed with up to fifty pounds of cargo. The Indians weren't heartless slave drivers, though. They frequently outfitted their dogs with rawhide booties to keep their paws from freezing in the snow.

Dogs were also an early warning system, barking to alert their people of intruders, whether it was a wolf or bear or a scout from a warring tribe. Many a tragedy was averted thanks to the insistent barking of the vigilant dogs.

Perhaps the most important partnership enjoyed by Sheepeater and dog was in hunting big game. Archaeologists have identified the remains of several complex sheep traps built where herds were known to congregate. Long "driveways" were constructed with deadfall, creating walls up to five feet high. Bighorn sheep were chased by dogs into a holding pen, where they were subsequently clubbed or killed with arrows by men hiding behind blinds they'd built out of rock. Like most successful hunters, the Sheepeaters had an intimate knowledge of their prey's behavior. The bighorn sheep inhabited rocky areas, but they loved to feed on the plants and grasses that were abundant in the lower-elevation meadows and draws between rock outcroppings. They rarely wandered more than a couple hundred yards from the rocks, and when they perceived a threat they would run to the outcrop, almost always uphill, to seek refuge. The Sheepeaters designed their traps accordingly, building ever-narrowing driveways that ran uphill toward the perceived safety of the rocks, where they would lie in wait, hidden in blinds near the holding pen. Downslope, when the herd appeared, several hunters and dogs would simply walk in full view of the sheep, making them nervous enough to gather into a tight group. Then the dogs would run barking toward the sheep, herding them into the driveway. The sheep, as predicted, ran uphill toward the rocks and their demise.

The Sheepeaters weren't the first to keep dogs, of course, but trappers who encountered these Mountain Shoshone frequently remarked on the well-behaved animals, in sharp contrast to their own dogs, which sometimes fought each other, ignored commands, and constantly had to be stopped from stealing food and chewing up leather goods.

Accounts of Sheepeaters that characterized them as ill suited for war were inaccurate and dumbed down. Pugnacious tribes like the Comanche and the Blackfeet captured the imagination of the nineteenth-century pioneer, who tended to stereotype all Indians as angry warriors eager to spill the white man's blood. Sheepeaters, being nomads, typically had no land to fight over. They were fully capable of protecting themselves from an attack but were not known to go looking for trouble. They tended to avoid conflict. Theirs was a relatively mellow existence with few horses or firearms to ratchet things up to a loud and dangerous level.

Like all Native Americans, the Sheepeaters fell victim to western expansion at the end of the 1800s. They ranged across a territory that provided a wide variety of food sources, including big game, berries, nuts, and roots. Fish were also a large part of their diet, but as gold miners infiltrated their territory, many streams became polluted and dammed, decimating fish populations. Beavers, too, were harvested nearly to extinction by trappers. Bison, bighorn sheep, elk, and deer were hunted relentlessly, thinning out a huge source of protein for the Sheepeaters. Not the most gregarious of Indian tribes to begin with, they became even more reclusive, avoiding contact with white people as well as other tribes as they had to work harder to find food. Since their response to encounters with explorers and hunters in Yellowstone was usually to flee, their behavior was misread as timorous. In a Wild West culture that featured men eager to let their guns do the talking, the Sheepeaters were branded as cowards.

Several mountain men and trappers from the earlier part of the 1800s tell a different story. While the Sheepeaters were wary of anyone, especially white men, coming into their territory, they were willing trade partners whose craftsmanship and expert tailoring produced items that were in great demand. Sir François Larocque of the Northwest Fur Company made one of the earliest reports on the Sheepeaters at a trading event on the Yellowstone River. He remarked on the fine quality of their tailored clothing, animal skins, horn bows, and obsidian preforms. Their negotiating skills, however, left a lot to be desired. At these early trading events, the Sheepeater artisans would simply toss their furs and other goods on the ground and wait for the traders to tell them what it was worth.

Along with intricately decorated buckskin shirts and dresses, the Sheepeaters created moccasins, boots, and coyote-skin caps. They also stitched together buckskin leggings from softened rawhide, featuring fur linings and fringe along the legs that would wick away water. The moccasins were constructed from badger hide or elk skin. These items weren't just produced as trading stock for the Europeans—a pair of knee-high Sheepeater boots, complete with sinew laces, was found in Mummy Cave and determined to have been made anywhere from AD 670 to 890.

As fine as the fit and finish was on their sartorial creations, the most highly prized item produced by the Sheepeaters is one that was rarely for sale. The hunting bows crafted from the massive horns of bighorn sheep were stunning works of art that were as powerful as they were beautiful. Wood bows carried by other Indians and European-American hunters didn't have the oomph to bring down large game, so the Sheepeaters turned to their favorite resource: the bighorn sheep. The process of making a bow was extremely laborious and time intensive, but they could produce weapons that were half the length of traditional wood longbows but had the same draw strength.

The bowmaker would start by soaking the horns in hot water, likely one of Yellowstone's numerous hot pools, to soften them up. This process was repeated several times, and then long strips of material would be removed from the horn's core, their casing scraped away with obsidian blades. The remaining horn staves were soaked a few more times, softened, and bound between two boards for seven to ten days. (All horn shavings, by the way, were saved for making into glue.) Once it was time to shape the bow—typically two or three lengths of horn joined together and bound with sinew—it would be shaped so that when drawn it would pull away from the natural curvature of the horn. Once the staves were joined with glue made from rendered horn shavings and sturgeon bladders, strips of sinew were attached along the length of the bow's outside curve. The sinew gave it flexibility and strength—without it, the bone would shatter under the tension. Thus fortified, the belly, or inside, of the bow could withstand more compression than wood. Sometimes a snakeskin was glued over the sinew, but this was purely for ornamentation. Occasionally buffalo or elk antlers were used, but sheep horn produced the most highly valued bows. And valuable they were. One mountain man, George Belden, was able to persuade a Sheepeater to sell him his horn bow for the princely sum of $32 in gold. That ounce and a half of gold would run you about $1,800 today.

Notches were carved into the bow's ends to hold the bowstring, which was made of twisted sinew. Most of the horn bows were just under three feet long, about the length of today's compound hunting bows. The arrows were long, though, typically as long as the bow. Bowmakers strove to make the arrows as straight as possible to take advantage of the horn bow's great accuracy. Greasewood, chokecherry, and red willow were all used. The shaft was straightened by drawing the branch between two rough rocks, or sometimes by using a "shaft wrench," a small hole drilled into a piece of horn. Lacking tools or proper rocks, some Sheepeaters just pulled the shafts between their teeth. These straightened shafts were then dried and cured for up to a year to get them to maximum strength. Four- to five-inch fletching (preferably owl or eagle feathers, which would not absorb blood) were lashed to the shaft with sinew. An obsidian or other rock point was attached to one end and a notch carved in the other, and it was hunting time.

Only one Sheepeater horn bow has been found in an archaeological context. Now on display in the Mountain Man Museum in Pinedale, Wyoming, the bow was unearthed in a cave in the Gros Ventre Mountains in western Wyoming. It was dated to 1737 and displays all the characteristics typical of a Sheepeater bow.

The brilliant craftsmanship of the horn bow is just one example of how adept the Sheepeaters were at using local resources to their utmost potential. When game was scarce they would catch fish and gather seeds, nuts, berries, and bugs. They adapted to the sometimes harsh environs of Yellowstone and thrived for generations, traveling light as they roamed from the high-altitude forests to the riverside hunting grounds. They'd been part of the mountain landscape for thousands of years. Once our first national park was designated, however, they would soon be forced out of their homeland. Philetus P. Norris, the park's second superintendent, lobbied Congress to exclude all Indians from the park. This included not only the Sheepeaters but also the Crow, Bannock, and other Shoshone bands that were known to occasionally live in the area.

Things came to a head during the Sheepeater Indian War of 1879, when a group of Sheepeaters were accused in the death of five Chinese gold miners near Challis, Idaho. It became evident later that they were not responsible for the deaths, but not before two detachments of US soldiers mounted a four-month campaign, eventually capturing fifty-one Indians. The Sheepeaters had managed to elude their captors several times, but finally their time in Yellowstone had come to an end. Most of the Mountain Shoshone were sent to the Wind River Reservation in Wyoming, while a few wound up on the Fort Hall Reservation near Pocatello, Idaho.

Today you can take a short hike from the eastern Grand Loop Road, about eight miles south of Mammoth Hot Springs, and check out Sheepeater Cliff. A short, unmarked trail leads past the forty-foot-tall wall of columnar basalt. The large, polygonal columns are reminiscent of those found on the Devils Tower in Wyoming. The cliffs were named by Philetus Norris in 1879 when he visited the area and saw several remnants of wickiups and assumed they belonged to the Sheepeaters. Pretty much every tribe in North America used wickiups, however, which were shelters made by stacking poles into a cone shape. Many tribes moved through Yellowstone in the mid-nineteenth century, and it's unlikely these belonged to the Sheepeaters.

Today the main inhabitants of the cliffs are yellow-bellied marmots, and it can be fun to take a picnic and watch the large, chirping rodents scamper around the rocks. Although the cliffs bear their name, it's not an area known to have been inhabited by the Sheepeaters. A short hike downstream takes you to another cliff wall and a view of Tukadeka Falls—again, not a place where Sheepeaters are known to have lived.

Misnomer aside, Sheepeater Cliff pays homage to a resourceful band of Shoshone Indians who were seldom seen and left little behind to tell their story. As time goes on, though, more sites are uncovered, producing more artifacts that offer some clues to this mysterious tribe who roamed Yellowstone thousands of years before the first white man ever "discovered" this preternatural wonderland.

CHAPTER 4

Yellowstone Lake's Mysterious Music

Something strange is going on at Yellowstone Lake. At nearly 132 square miles, it's the largest alpine lake in North America. Its 141 miles of shoreline sit almost a mile and a half above sea level, and depths range as far as 400 feet. It's big. It's so big that summertime storms can create waves that look like they belong in the sea, not in a freshwater lake. This brawny, beautiful body of water is one of Yellowstone's most popular destinations, and its charms are many. But there's one feature of the lake that isn't talked about much: Yellowstone Lake makes sounds. Weird sounds. Check out this account from a visitor: "While getting breakfast, we heard every few moments a curious sound, between a whistle and a horse whine, whose locality and character we could not at first determine. The sound increased in force, and it now became evident that gusts of wind were passing through the air above us, though the pines did not as yet indicate the least motion in the lower atmosphere."

Fanciful story from an attention-starved tourist with an overactive imagination? Hardly. This was the report of respected geologist Frank H. Bradley, a member of the famed Hayden Expedition of 1871, the year before Yellowstone was designated a national park.

The odd noises have been heard by many for hundreds of years and are variously described as sounding like a flock of ducks in flight, metal cables crashing together, a swarm of bees, whistling, rumbling, dreamy organ music, and more. Most reports say that the sounds seem to emanate from the lake itself and move quickly through the air overhead. While dozens of theories have been bandied about over the years, there has never been a satisfying, scientific explanation.

What secrets are being whispered by Yellowstone Lake?

When there's a question about Yellowstone National Park, the best bet for a definitive answer is usually Lee H. Whittlesey, Yellowstone's official historian and author of at least a dozen books examining various aspects of the park and its history. A greater repository of Yellowstone knowledge you are not likely to find, but even Whittlesey comes up blank when asked to explain the weird sounds coming from Yellowstone Lake. "I first read about the mysterious Yellowstone Lake sounds in 1971," he said in an interview with the Travel Channel. "I was intrigued. Enthralled, in fact. To this day, nobody has a satisfactory explanation. We just don't know what causes that ethereal sound. But it is spooky. It has a paranormal, preternatural, supernatural element to it that is intriguing."

Spooky and *paranormal* are a couple of words favored by a certain corner of the investigative world that tends to chalk up mysterious occurrences to otherworldly sources. One oft-repeated theory of the lake's unexplained sounds is that the souls who drowned there are trapped in its depths and calling out from some watery purgatory. Whittlesey puts zero stock in the "ghosts and spirits" theory, but he's heard too many reports over the years to write it off as a Bigfoot-style myth. The sounds are real.

It's not hard to understand why some folks latch onto the idea that the ethereal noises are coming from beyond the grave. It's been said that Yellowstone Lake never gives up its dead. Since 1894, forty-one drownings there have been documented, and seventeen of those victims were never recovered. Where did those bodies go? One theory has to do with the physical characteristics of the lake. Despite sitting on top of an active volcano, the average temperature of the water hovers around forty degrees Fahrenheit. That's enough to cause hypothermia-induced unconsciousness in as little as thirty minutes. Once the symptoms of sluggishness and mental haze set in, usually within a few minutes, chances of survival drop pretty quickly. Even if a person could keep themselves afloat in the lake, they would succumb to hypothermia long before they would drown. Once the victim slips under the surface, the cold water replaces air in the lungs, robbing the body of its buoyancy. When the water is cold enough, as in Yellowstone Lake, it also prevents bacteria-produced gases from forming in the body, which would usually cause it to rise to the surface. This probably explains why some drowning victims were never found, but it certainly doesn't explain the spooky sounds.

The unique geology and topographical quirks of Yellowstone Park provide fodder for some ideas about what might be producing the mysterious "lake music." A *Popular Mechanics* article from 1930 suggests that the sounds may originate from the echoes of earthquakes beneath the lake. Yellowstone is hit by anywhere from one thousand to three thousand earthquakes per year, most too mild to be felt. Occasionally, though, "earthquake swarms" strike the area beneath the lake bottom, serving up hundreds of quakes in a single day. This activity, opined the article's author, could be creating sound waves in the underground gaps and caverns beneath the lake bottom, which are then amplified by a temperature inversion above the lake. This theory has never been proven. Another theory, put forth by ranger naturalist Neil Miner, suggests that air flowing down over the lake from nearby mountain peaks could create swirling vortices that somehow produce an audible hum. This theory handily explains why the sounds are also sometimes reportedly heard at nearby Shoshone Lake to the southwest.

None of these quasi-scientific suggestions have satisfied experts. The possibility is always there that the sounds are just odd confluences of ambient noise or even the products of suggestible tourists visiting the park. That seems unlikely, though, since many of these reports have come from some reputable sources who had nothing to gain from sensationalizing such a claim. Hiram Chittenden, the highly respected historian and engineer whose influence on the park is still apparent today, wrote an official account of the Yellowstone Lake hum in his 1895 book, *The Yellowstone National Park: Historical and Descriptive*: "A most singular and interesting acoustic phenomenon of the region, although rarely noticed by tourists is the occurrence of strange and indefinable overhead sounds. They have long been noted by explorers, but only in the vicinity of Shoshone and Yellowstone Lakes. They seem to occur in the morning and last only a moment." Chittenden was a methodical man of science and engineering, not given to flights of fancy or unsubstantiated stories.

Legendary guide Elwood "Billy" Hofer had also heard the sounds, and the experienced denizen of the Yellowstone plateau

View looking north over Yellowstone Lake from West Thumb. Mysterious sounds from the lake have been reported for more than one hundred years.

EDNOR THERRIAULT.

was at a loss to explain its origin, calling it "the most mysterious sound heard among the mountains." Geologists, rangers, naturalists, scientists, and professors have all published accounts of hearing the weird noises over Yellowstone Lake, but we are still waiting for substantive proof as to its origin.

Unless, of course, it's a secret government program. As with most unexplained phenomena, there is an army of conspiracy buffs who are convinced that that nebulous entity known only as "the government" is behind many unexplained mysteries, from Bigfoot to alien abductions. In the case of Yellowstone's lake music, however, they actually have a specific organization in mind.

The High Frequency Active Auroral Research Program, or HAARP, was a research endeavor begun in 1993, funded by the US Air Force, the US Navy, the University of Alaska Fairbanks, and the Defense Advanced Research Projects Agency. The purpose of the program was to explore and analyze the ionosphere with an eye toward developing enhanced radio technology and surveillance. The facility went fully online in 2007 when it completed its 180-antenna array, which yielded an effective radiated power of 5.1 gigawatts (more than four times the amount of energy needed for Doc Brown's flux capacitor in *Back to the Future*). The research station is located at a US Air Force site near Gakona, Alaska.

What could this possibly have to do with weird sounds over Yellowstone Lake, you ask? According to the tinfoil hat set, the culprit is an instrument developed by the program. The unimaginatively named Ionospheric Research Instrument (IRI) is a high-powered radio frequency transmitter that operates in the high frequency band. The IRI is used to excite an area within the ionosphere, and a host of other instruments are used to examine the effects on the area. It also, according to geoscientists, can generate a super low-frequency hum, similar to what's been described at Yellowstone Lake. Could this somehow be the source of the mysterious lake music? It's a stretch, but the conspiracy crowd doesn't stop there. This manipulation of the ionosphere, some say, can be used to affect the weather, even turning it into a weapon. Besides earthquakes, floods, hurricanes, and swapping the earth's magnetic poles, HAARP can be used to create strange sounds that seem to be coming from the sky. One proponent of this theory even claims that HAARP is a mind control device. He took a crew to visit the facility to get some answers. He was turned away. You might have heard of him: he's Jesse Ventura, the ex-governor of Minnesota.

Journalists, scientists, and university professors have thoroughly debunked claims that HAARP can in any way influence the weather, neutralize satellites, or trap the souls of people, as some have stated. Similar facilities are operational in Puerto Rico, Norway, and Russia. Like HAARP, none have been proven to be the source of any mystery sounds in Yellowstone Park or anywhere else.

Interestingly, the lake sounds seem to be heard more frequently in the winter months. Winter in Yellowstone is a harsh but gorgeous world, one that should be experienced at least once by all park enthusiasts. Travel is, of course, a different proposition than in the summer. There are several concessioners who run tours in the winter, and their tank-tread snowcats carry packs of tourists over massive snowdrifts and icy roads with ease. One road, from Mammoth to Cooke City, remains open year-round, and a limited number of interpretive and protective rangers spend the winter there. Yellowstone Lake is a quiet, white-on-white wonderland. The Yellowstone Lake Hotel is buttoned up for the season, and pretty much the only activity in the heart of the park is wildlife trudging through the snow, searching for food, although you can also see a few hardy snowshoers and cross-country skiers. The lake freezes over in the winter, except in the areas where hydrothermal vents release superheated water. The freeze usually starts in mid-December, and the thaw comes in late May to early June. The ice on the lake gets up to three feet thick, and several feet of snow are typically blanketed over it.

Anyone who's spent time on a sizable lake in the winter has probably heard the wild noises it makes when the ice cracks. From high-pitched pings that sound like a *Star Wars* light saber battle to subsonic groans that you can feel in your gut, the sounds are all over the sonic map. Also, as in many reported cases of the Yellowstone Lake mystery sounds, they seem to move as they develop. Could this be a partial explanation of Yellowstone's lake music?

Lake ice doesn't just freeze solid and sit on top of the water like a lid on a soup pot. It's dynamic—even the smallest changes in temperature cause the ice to expand or contract, and the resulting tension causes cracks to race across the ice. The resulting sounds vary according to several factors. The thickness of the ice, how long it's been frozen, the size of the lake, and how much snow covers the ice all affect the sound frequency of the cracking noise. If the ice is thin, it's more elastic and can vibrate more freely, like the head of a drum. This causes sounds to travel farther. Also, louder sounds cause the soundwaves to propagate more, causing sounds of varying volume to travel at different speeds, giving the illusion of movement.

The bigger the change in temperature, the more cracking there is, and more noises are heard. In the summer, visitors to the park enjoy pleasant days that get as warm as the low eighties, and then the nights cool off, with the mercury dropping into the forties, or even the upper thirties at higher elevations. That's a pretty wide swing, but in the winter it's even more dramatic. Daytime temperatures typically reach the teens and twenties, but a cold snap in the mountains can drop the temperature as much as seventy degrees. The lowest recorded temperature in Yellowstone Park is minus sixty-six degrees Fahrenheit. That's pretty snappy. When there's that much of a temperature fluctuation working on the thick slab of ice that covers Yellowstone Lake, there's lots of movement. The shifts and cracks can sound like giant icebergs grinding against each other. And if the layer of snow on top of the ice is not particularly deep, the noises will be louder and carry farther. In winter, at least, the wild and wacky noises caused by the movement of ice on the lake might account for some of the strange sounds that have been reported over the years.

What did Yellowstone's earliest visitors think of the lake music? Surely some Indians must have heard the weird noises coming off the massive lake as they moved through the park en route to the hunting grounds of eastern Wyoming and Montana over the last several thousand years. This is a question that's hard to answer, as it's tough to find solid information on what the Indians thought of the Yellowstone area in general. Historians can offer little but conjecture, as the many tribes who are known to have spent time in the area, from the Shoshone and Bannock to the Crow and Sheepeaters, have offered to share few stories of Yellowstone with people descended from the European-American wave that displaced their people in the 1800s. One thing we do know is that the widely accepted (and in some cases promoted) belief that Indians feared the Yellowstone area with its geysers and steam vents has been proven false. Indians did not avoid the park. In fact, archaeological evidence has shown that dozens of tribes moved through Yellowstone, the earliest being Paleo-Indians around thirteen thousand years ago. If anything, Indians saw Yellowstone as the home of benevolent spirits. There are indications that tribal members centered their vision quests and other ceremonies on the area's hydrothermal features.

But what about those sounds around Yellowstone Lake? Other than a Kiowa legend about the creation of Yellowstone Lake, there's scant information about any Indian encounters with the unexplained sounds that have been reported over the lake.

Whatever causes the Yellowstone Lake mystery noises, their variety teases the imagination of those who have heard it. Dr. Edwin Linton, who visited the lake in 1892, compared the noises to "a medley of wind in the tree tops . . . the echo of bells after being repeated several times, the humming of a swarm of bees, and two or three other less definite sources of sound, making in all a composite which was not loud, but easily recognized, and not at all likely to be mistaken for any other sound in these mountain solitudes."

Scientist S. A. Forbes also heard the lake music during a trip to the park in 1893. His account, like most, is unique in many ways but shares a few characteristics with other reports, like the way the sound seems to move, usually going north to south. "It put me in mind of the vibrating clang of a harp lightly and rapidly touched high up above the tree tops." He also described it as sounding like several telegraph wires vibrating in the wind, adding that the sound of faint voices could be heard overhead. Perhaps others heard what sounded like voices as well, lending to the myth that these sounds were the despairing cries of those who had drowned in the lake.

The lake sounds were reported by geologist Clyde Max Bauer, the park's chief naturalist, who wrote about his experiences in his book *Yellowstone: The Underworld*. He heard the sounds many times in the 1930s, describing them as the ringing of telegraph wires or the humming of bees. The sounds would begin softly in the distance and increase in volume as they seemed to pass overhead, subsequently fading as they moved away. He also recorded the experiences of park ranger Verde Watson, who heard the sounds nearly every morning in 1933 while working as a caretaker at the Lake Museum.

Since the 1930s reports of people hearing sounds on Yellowstone Lake have dropped off, but that doesn't mean they've gone away. Whittlesey postulates that people just don't like to talk about it. As with Sasquatch sightings or UFO encounters, people who claim to hear mysterious noises tend to keep it to themselves rather than be viewed as someone who might have a screw loose. Consequently, it's become a little-known phenomenon in the park.

"You have to have a real interest in Yellowstone history to even be familiar with it," said Whittlesey. "There are a number of pieces written about it, but it's often buried deep in the literature." Although Yellowstone's crack historian has listened for the sounds for several years—any time he's camped in the backcountry near Shoshone Lake or Yellowstone Lake—he has yet to hear them with his own ears. Still, with so many firsthand accounts from such reputable sources as his early predecessor, Hiram Chittenden, Whittlesey doesn't dismiss the existence of the lake music. Like those who have heard it, he just hasn't found a credible explanation. "It has been reported by too many people for it to be any kind of Bigfoot thing or something like that."

These ethereal sounds that whoosh by overhead at Yellowstone Lake—are they the product of some underground activity being amplified through the icy waters of the lake? Are they the sound of air moving as it comes off the nearby peaks? Is this just the ominous sound created by lake ice cracking and flexing in the winter? Theories and possible explanations abound, but none have definitively answered the question of the lake's odd music. Perhaps science will one day catch up to the elusive cause of the mystery sounds, but for now it remains one of Yellowstone's enduring legends. Pay close attention the next time you're spending time around Yellowstone Lake. Perhaps you'll be lucky enough to hear the park's big blue jewel whisper a few secrets in your ear.

CHAPTER 5

The Devil's Kitchenette

Early explorers who stumbled into Yellowstone were dumbfounded—and probably a little frightened—by the terrifying beauty of the place. The roaring geysers, brightly colored hot pools, steaming fissures, and other dramatic features could only have sprung forth from hell itself, spurring those who saw them to assign names that alluded to the netherworld. John Colter, one of the first European Americans to set foot in the area, sent descriptions back East, but "Colter's Hell" was thought to be a tall tale, too fantastic to be true. "The place where hell bubbled up" (mountain man Jim Bridger's succinct description of the area) led to such names as Hell's Gate Spring, Hell Broth Springs, Hellroaring Creek, and Hell's Half Acre. Old Scratch himself would have felt right at home wandering around the Devil's Den, the Devil's Thumb, the Devil's Breath, the Devil's Gate, and the Devil's Punch Bowl.

As science began to overtake emotion in the Gilded Age of the late nineteenth century, satanic-themed nomenclature began to fade. In the early twentieth century, though, the Devil's Kitchenette appeared—a man-made attraction that enjoyed a brief but successful run in Mammoth Hot Springs. The cleverly named Devil's Kitchenette represents an important piece of the park's history. The small luncheonette built near a steaming crack in the earth known as the Devil's Kitchen was part of one of the most successful dynasties to do business in the park's first century. Two sisters, Anna Pryor and Elizabeth Trischman, spent forty years overcoming the obstacles of two world wars, the Great Depression, stubborn gender politics, and unspeakable family tragedy to parlay a small curio shop in Mammoth Hot Springs into a sprawling enterprise that included nearly all concessions in the northern end of the park. The Pryor-Trischman dynasty has been somewhat buried in the sands of time, but it's one of Yellowstone's most engaging legends that just happens to be true.

George Trischman emigrated from Germany to the United States at an interesting time in our history. The Civil War had just ended, and a battle-weary country looked westward, where wide-open expanses of new territory fired the imaginations of thousands of people seeking a new start after the ravages of war. It was 1866. The US Army also moved westward seeking to secure the land. Trischman, a carpenter and wheelwright, joined the army and was stationed at Fort Shaw, Montana.

In 1883 he found a bride, Margaret. Their first child, Anna, was born the following year. The family added four more children while at Fort Custer, including Elizabeth (born with twin brother Harry in 1886) and Joseph, the baby of the family. As schools were lacking at the post, Margaret and the children lived in nearby Billings. When Fort Custer closed in 1898, George rejoined his family. The happy reunion, however, would soon give way to an episode so horrific that it made national news.

On a spring day in 1899, Margaret selected a large butcher knife from the kitchen and went to a cow shed on the property, where she attempted suicide by slashing her throat. She missed her jugular, however, and survived, explaining the large gash in her neck with a story of being attacked by another woman. She recuperated at home for a few weeks, her husband keeping a close eye on her. One day, when he left to run an errand, he returned to find Margaret gone. She was eventually located on an island in the middle of the Yellowstone River near the Northern Pacific Railroad bridge. A few days later, on the recommendation of two doctors and a judge, Margaret was committed to the Montana asylum at Warm Springs. George, meanwhile, had taken a job at Fort Yellowstone as a post carpenter. Apparently, the pressure of raising five children on his own became too much to bear, and six weeks after her commitment George arranged for Margaret's release from Warm Springs, even though her doctor there said she'd made no progress in the treatment of her "melancholia."

The family settled into their new home in Mammoth Hot Springs, but it was just a few days before Margaret snapped. She once again grabbed a knife and used it to cut the throat of her youngest son. Five-year-old Joseph was nearly decapitated, and Margaret went after the rest of the kids. They were able to flee to a neighbor's house, where the authorities were summoned. They found Margaret at home, no doubt covered in blood. It was reported that she was disoriented and oblivious to the vicious crime she'd committed. Word of the shocking tragedy at Fort Yellowstone quickly spread. The *New York Times* ran an account of the slaying, reporting that Margaret was "undoubtedly insane." She was charged with murder and, since it had occurred on federal land, was ordered to be committed to an asylum in Washington, DC. George and a federal marshal placed Margaret on a train at Cinnabar, but somewhere in the Paradise Valley she jumped off the train, almost certainly into the Yellowstone River. No trace of her was ever found.

George was devastated. That autumn he sent the four surviving children to Helena to attend school. After her graduation, Anna returned to Fort Yellowstone to work as a schoolteacher. It was there that she met George Pryor, and they were married in an elaborate church wedding in Gardiner. Anna's lifelong affinity for Yellowstone Park was only just beginning.

The colorful travertine terraces at Mammoth Hot Springs are a surreal vision of smooth plateaus and tiered shelves created by minerals flowing through the superheated waters of underground springs for thousands of years. The spectacular series of geothermal formations is a popular Yellowstone destination, an eye-popping welcome for visitors entering the park through Gardiner. In the early days of the park, tourists would frequently submerge items into the gently flowing waters of the terraces until they were coated with minerals, giving them a nifty souvenir to take home. Ole Anderson capitalized on the practice by opening a tent souvenir stand that he called the Specimen House at the base of the Mammoth terraces. He did a brisk business selling mineral-coated bottles, pine cones, toys, combs, and other trinkets for more than twenty years. Eventually his tent gave way to a permanent structure, and in 1908 he decided to retire and accepted an offer from Anna and George Pryor to buy his business.

The Pryors, seeing opportunity, immediately requested permission from the Department of Interior to sell ice cream, cold drinks, and pastries at the stand. They were not only granted a permit but also allowed to make the Specimen House their residence. Their inventory soon grew to include penny postcards, bottles of colored sand from Yellowstone's Grand Canyon, and other tourist doo-dads. To reflect their variety of offerings, they renamed the business the Park Curio Shop.

Anna's sister Elizabeth finished school and came to Mammoth to help the couple run the store. By 1910 Anna and George had two girls, Georganna and Margaret. Their shop was doing a booming business, now selling even more cosmopolitan goods such as Indian moccasins and Mexican blankets.

Trouble was bubbling to the surface, however, in their beautiful little corner of Yellowstone. The lives of the two sisters took a major turn in 1912 when George and Anna's marriage fell apart. George signed over his interest in the business, and Anna and Elizabeth created the partnership of Pryor and Trischman. George appeared to make plans to stay at Mammoth, applying for a permit to run a herd of dairy cows. He never went through with it, though, and left the area. Anna, her two daughters, and sister Elizabeth forged ahead with the Park Curio Shop. Business was so good, in fact, that they applied for a permit to open a refreshment stand near a subterranean thermal pool on the upper terraces known as the Devil's Kitchen. The Devil's Kitchenette, they proposed, would offer cool drinks and ice cream to adventurous visitors who had the guts to climb down a long wooden ladder into this steaming gash in the earth. Their application was denied, as authorities thought the refreshment stand would be too close to the geothermal feature, presenting a possible hazard to park visitors. The sisters kept the idea in their back pocket, awaiting another opportunity.

Competition heated up in the spring of 1913 when George Whittaker bought the Mammoth general store, renaming it the Yellowstone Park Store. He sold much of what the sisters offered, as well as Kodak film, hardware, groceries, and sporting goods. It was like seeing Walmart move in next to their mom-and-pop store, but the sisters were undaunted. When Whittaker applied for a permit to open a soda fountain, Anna and Elizabeth countered by applying for permission to sell Kodak film and other sundry goods. Acting superintendent Colonel Lloyd Brett, sensing an ugly commerce war brewing, wisely denied both applications.

The two businesses managed to coexist for the next couple of years, until the park lifted its ban on automobiles in 1915. By now the sisters had their own soda fountain and had doubled the size of the Park Curio Shop. Like their competitor Whittaker, they saw the imminent market for all things automotive and applied for permission to open a gas station. Whittaker's application was approved; the sisters' was denied. Still, they were unbowed. Their growing business now had five employees, and the 1915 season produced a profit of $3,167 for Anna and Elizabeth—an impressive sum at a time when an ice cream cone cost fifteen cents.

The following year would usher in more big changes as the National Park Service (NPS) was created to manage the growing number of national parks. Also, the United States' entry into World

War I had pulled all available soldiers from their post at Fort Yellowstone. The NPS wasted no time in flexing its muscle. Director Stephen T. Mather, feeling that there were too many businesses competing for small slivers of the Yellowstone tourist pie, wanted to reduce the number of companies working in the park. At the end of 1915, when their lease came up for renewal for the 1916 season, Anna and Elizabeth were given only a one-year contract. Some would have seen the writing on the wall and perhaps thrown in the towel, but the sisters doubled down, gaining permission to further expand their offerings to include newspapers, toiletries, tobacco, and box lunches. Fortunately for the Pryor-Trischman team, the NPS was focused on hotels and transportation companies, and the sisters avoided any major shakeup to their business. The next year they were given a ten-year lease.

Although visitor numbers were down in the summer of 1917—likely due to the war—the sisters ran a lean operation and were able to weather the slow times. At the end of the season, though, their business was further squeezed when the park closed down twenty days early in anticipation of a threatened Northern Pacific strike. US commissioner Judge John W. Meldrum wrote, "Within 50 hours after the decision [to close the park early] every employee and tourist had left the park." The truncated season amounted to a thousand dollars in lost sales for the sisters. Their reaction? They spent $1,100 on a brand-new Buick.

Anna's older daughter, Georganna, was almost ten years old by then, so Anna and her girls wintered in Great Falls, where they could attend school. Elizabeth had begun spending her winters living in Helena, working as a clerk for the legislature. By 1917 she

had become the chief clerk in the office of the House of Represen-
tatives. Judge Meldrum, their neighbor in Mammoth, had become
a close friend, going on road trips and celebrating holidays with the
Pryor-Trischman family, especially after his wife, Emmaline, died in
1908. He even got the chance to play Santa Claus for Anna's daughters at their Mammoth home, thrilling the girls by appearing in a
custom-made Santa suit with a sack full of dolls and a large, fully
furnished doll house. Georganna later remarked to her mother how
similar Santa's voice was to that of their friend, Judge Meldrum.

Summers continued to be profitable for the sisters, tallying
gross sales of $24,000 for the 1922 season. Their friendly rivalry
with George Whittaker became a partnership when they teamed up
to open an "experimental delicatessen stand" in the free auto camp
at Lower Mammoth. Auto camps had sprung up around the park,
affording tourists the opportunity to spend time in the park and see
the sights at their own pace rather than being shepherded around
on tour buses and wagons. Things were going so well that Anna and
Elizabeth decided to take another run at the Devil's Kitchenette.

This time the answer was yes.

The secretary of the interior granted the sisters a one-year
permit allowing them to operate the snack counter near the Devil's
Kitchen. The Devil's Kitchenette debuted during the 1924 season
and quickly became almost as popular as the thermal cavern itself.
Part of the success, one would think, was due to the clever name. It's
hard to believe that Satan's Snack Bar would have been as popular.
Nonalcoholic drinks and ice cream flew out the window, snapped
up by tourists who developed a powerful thirst while climbing
down a long rickety ladder, dodging bats as they descended into

The Devil's Kitchenette on the Mammoth Hot Springs upper terrace, owned and operated by the Pryor-Trischman sisters.

the large, steamy underground vault. The following year the Devil's Kitchenette was written into the annual permit with the rest of the Pryor-Trischman businesses.

Yellowstone's growing crowds had big appetites, and the enterprising sisters were eager to feed them. In 1925 they persuaded George Whittaker to sell them his interest in the auto camp delicatessen, which they immediately expanded by adding a range and steam table, fully equipping the facility to serve cafeteria-style meals. By this time they had three locations, and each sister was paid an annual salary of $12,000. They'd doubled the size of their Park Curio Shop—again—and had sixteen employees, including seventeen-year-old Georganna. In a letter to his niece, Judge Meldrum wrote, "If you shouldn't think that these women are 'captains of finance,' you have another guess coming to you."

Their business thriving, Anna and Elizabeth followed the lead of many of their fellow concessioners and bought a house in Los Angeles, where they began to spend their winters. In the fall of 1927 they threw an extravagant birthday party for the judge, who was turning eighty-four. They also celebrated his status as the oldest living resident of Yellowstone Park. The guest list for the party, which was held at the Grand Canyon Hotel, included such park luminaries as Superintendent Horace Albright and park photographer Jack Haynes. The generosity of the two sisters seemed to know no bounds, and they certainly didn't display any trepidation about the continued success of the Pryor-Trischman enterprise.

Then Black Friday happened. The stock market crash of 1929 pitched the entire country into a downward economic spiral that would affect everyone. Somehow Anna and Elizabeth managed to avoid catastrophe in the summer after the crash, but the following year, 1931, would be the first time their business had ever shown a loss. They responded by tightening their belts and cutting their own salaries down to almost nothing. The stock market collapse came on the heels of the death of their father, George, in May. He died in Sawtelle, California, at the National Home for Disabled Volunteer Soldiers, at age eighty, but he'd lived long enough to see his daughters buck the odds to become successful entrepreneurs who were able to enjoy the fruits of their hard work. The sisters grieved, but this wouldn't be their last heartache. In 1930 Anna's daughter Margaret died after a two-year illness. After she was laid to rest in Los Angeles, Anna and Elizabeth mustered the strength to return to their Yellowstone enterprise, which was facing the challenge of declining business in the ongoing Great Depression.

Their shrewd business acumen and penchant for plowing money back into their company paid off, allowing the sisters to emerge from the Great Depression relatively unscathed. While most of the country was reeling from the economic disaster and queuing up in bread lines, Pryor-Trischman was angling to buy out the competition. Their old Mammoth rival George Whittaker was sixty-two and eyeing retirement, which did not escape the sisters' notice. They offered him $75,000 for his retail operations in Mammoth and Canyon. Whitaker had learned that running a business in Yellowstone could be a prickly process, and he didn't want to sell out only to see his hard-won business run into the ground. However, knowing that Anna and Elizabeth were old hands at dealing with the shifting policies of the NPS and the park administration, Whittaker was happy to take them up on their offer. After securing loans from the

Yellowstone Transportation Company and the National Park Bank in Livingston, Anna traveled to Washington, DC, to negotiate the transfer of Whittaker's lease to Pryor-Trischman. The new lease prohibited them from selling photographic equipment or supplies due to the exclusive contract that had been awarded to Haynes Picture Shops. They hardly shed tears over this development—the sisters now owned the Park Curio Shop, three stores, two gas stations, a deli/cafeteria, and the Devil's Kitchenette. The entire north-end territory of Yellowstone Park was theirs.

By the end of the 1930s the crowds began to return. In their retail outlets, the sisters were now offering pretty much anything visitors could want, including liquor, beer, and wine. In 1939 they advertised a five-course Sunday meal for seventy-five cents. In 1941 Pryor-Trischman received a new lease for their concessions, this time for a period of twenty years. They'd proven themselves to the NPS, to their fellow concessioners, and to anyone who doubted that two women could have taken over a single souvenir shop and grown it into an enterprise that would thrive in the face of so many obstacles. That year Yellowstone Park topped half a million visitors, with 580,000 visiting the western wonderland. When the United States was pulled into World War II after Pearl Harbor, however, the number of visitors once again plummeted. By 1944 only 64,000 visitors per year came to the park.

Even the seemingly untouchable business of the Pryor-Trischman sisters suffered from this decline in tourist numbers. They were forced to close the Park Curio Shop in Mammoth, as well as the deli/cafeteria and store at the Lower Mammoth Auto Camp. In fact, they had to shutter every business except for the Mammoth General Store and their gas stations. They began to consider the option of retirement and restructured their partnership into a corporation. That way, if one sister died, the other wouldn't have to go through the permitting process all over again.

A life of leisure in sunny California beckoned, but they had trouble finding a suitable buyer for their business, which had begun to bounce back in the post-war economic boom. The tourists returned, and Yellowstone topped a million visitors in 1948. Sales for the 1952 season for Pryor Stores, Inc. hit a new high of $383,406.26. Anna and Elizabeth decided to go out on top. They negotiated a deal with Charles Hamilton, who owned most of the stores in the south end of the park, and sold their business for $300,000, dissolving their corporation in March 1953.

The sisters at last were able to retire to their Los Angeles home, where the post-war paradise of Southern California suited them quite well. Anna's life was once again shattered, however, when her daughter Georganna died from a series of strokes in 1961. She was fifty-three.

Anna died in Los Angeles in 1973 at the age of eighty-nine, and her sister and partner followed in 1984, passing away at ninety-seven.

The Devil's Kitchenette operated for fourteen years, shutting down just a couple of years before the park roped off the entrance to the Devil's Kitchen, proclaiming it too dangerous for visitors. The legacy of Anna and Elizabeth lives on, however, as a wonderful example of success through hard work, perseverance, and an ability to roll with the punches. In the sometimes wild and woolly early days of Yellowstone Park, this was a hard-won prize indeed. And for two women to have achieved this despite the prejudice of sexism that we're still seeing, well, success must have tasted that much sweeter.

CHAPTER 6

The Ghosts of Old Faithful Inn

Creepy apparitions, unexplained occurrences, and things that go bump in the night are constantly scaring the bejesus out of people all over the world, and why should Yellowstone Park be any different? Every year there are a few visitors to the park, perfectly rational people, who swear up and down that they've had an encounter with a spirit, witnessed objects moving around on their own, or soiled their jammies over a late-night glimpse of some spectral entity. Dating back to the 1800s, these reports have been a small but constant part of the Yellowstone experience. We're still waiting for hard evidence to prove the existence of any visitors from the afterlife, but there are a few stories that persist in Yellowstone folklore, and a handful of alleged ghosts are reportedly seen in the same areas. Why are some of the park's visitors claiming to see the same things, and how did these stories get started in the first place?

Yellowstone has seen its share of tragedy. Fatal mishaps resulting from some of the park's natural hazards happen all too frequently when visitors either disregard commonsense safety rules or find themselves in the wrong place at the wrong time. And the darker side of humanity is evident in the random suicide or murder that takes place here. Some believe that the spirits of those who met their end in Yellowstone tend to hang around, making their presence known through harmless pranks, or perhaps just putting their melancholy on display near the location of their demise. While some of the oft-told ghost stories are good for a few campfire chills, a number of these legends have their roots in far more nefarious events.

The Old Faithful Inn almost looks like it was designed to be haunted. The eighty-five-foot-tall structure, the largest log building in the world, was designed by renowned architect Robert C. Reamer. His use of locally sourced building materials like lodgepole pine and rough rhyolite rock contributed to a rugged style that became known as National Park Service rustic. The inn's seven stories tower over a broad lobby dominated by a massive stone fireplace that reaches to the roof. Guest rooms wrap around the perimeter, balconies overlooking the cavernous interior. The log work throughout is beautifully intricate, the clever design providing support for the massive structure that's stood for more than a hundred years. It even survived the infamous Yellowstone earthquake of 1959, a magnitude 7.5 temblor, although much of the chimney crumbled. These days visitors are not allowed to ascend past the balcony on the third floor, which means that you can't walk all the way up the wooden stairs to the odd little structure called the crow's nest, a railed platform suspended near the ceiling, seventy-six feet above the floor of the lobby. In the early days of the inn, string quartets or small bands would squeeze into the crow's nest and entertain the throngs of tourists milling below. Over the years a number of Old Faithful Inn guests and even a few staff members have reported seeing, usually late at night, a woman in a flowing white dress moving across the crow's nest, stopping to look down over the rail. In most of these accounts, she is holding her decapitated head under her arm.

The year was 1915. The United States was still five years away from giving women the right to vote, Babe Ruth hit his first career home run that summer, and the nation's first stop sign appeared in Detroit. Yellowstone National Park was forty-three years old. In San Francisco, the Panama-Pacific International Exposition opened, featuring a full-on reproduction of the Old Faithful Inn. The plaster-and-burlap replica would be razed by year's end, but not before people got an eyeful of the stunning hotel that awaited them in Yellowstone Park, then considered an exotic destination for the well heeled. The year 1915 also happened to be the first year that automobiles were allowed into the park.

Also that summer, a teenage heiress from New York was to be married. Her father, a wealthy shipping magnate, had arranged her marriage to the son of another well-to-do family. But, alas, the rebellious young spitfire was in love with another man. The object of her affection was much older, a servant in her family's household. Her father implored her to forget about the older fellow, whom he was convinced was marrying his daughter to get his hands on the family's wealth. The young woman held her ground, though, and refused to go through with the arranged marriage. Like most fathers, this one had a weakness when it came to his daughter, and he capitulated. There was a catch, however: he would present the couple with a hefty dowry as a wedding gift, but after that she would be cut off from the family fortune, and the servant would be cut loose from his employ. This, the father thought, would surely cause the gold digger to pull the plug on the couple's wedding plans. Again he was wrong. The young couple went through with their wedding and traveled west to Yellowstone Park for their honeymoon. The young bride was faced with a rude awakening, however, when the husband began spending their nest egg recklessly, gambling and drinking at taverns along the way. By the time they arrived at the Old Faithful Inn, their relationship was strained and their wedding bankroll was getting thin. Nevertheless, they checked into Room 127.

A month into their honeymoon, the money ran out. The couple argued loudly and frequently in their room, overheard by the hotel staff. Realizing that her father had been right about her husband, the young bride phoned home and asked for enough money to cover their hotel bill. She was denied. One night the staff heard the couple's fighting grow even louder in their room, the sounds of violent scuffling booming through the door. Shortly afterward the husband emerged from Room 127 and slammed the door behind him. He left the Old Faithful Inn and was never seen again.

Rather than intrude on the young woman, the staff decided to allow her some privacy, giving her time to collect herself. When a couple of days went by and she hadn't left the room, they became concerned and entered the room to check on her. The place was in shambles. Clothing and bedding was strewn about, the aftermath of an epic battle. The bride was nowhere to be seen. When a hotel maid walked into the bathroom, however, her blood-curdling scream brought everyone running, fearing the worst. There was the young woman, sprawled in the bathtub, drenched in blood. She had been decapitated. Staff members frantically searched the immediate area, but her head could not be found.

Days later, guests began to complain of a foul odor in the hotel. It seemed to be coming from the crow's nest, high up near the ceiling of the lobby. Someone was sent up to the tiny platform to take a look, and, to his horror, there lay the young woman's severed head.

Old Faithful Inn tour guides are reluctant to tell this story, but suggestible guests of the venerable hotel who have heard the tale still occasionally claim to see the figure of a young woman in a bridal dress drifting around the place, carrying her head under her arm like a halfback cradling a football.

It's a grisly story, probably the most well-known tale of murder told in Yellowstone Park. And it's total claptrap. Every word of it.

George Bornemann, at the time an assistant manager of the Old Faithful complex, told the *Deseret News* in a 1991 interview

Bedroom similar to Room 127 in the Old Faithful Inn, supposed location of the 1915 murder of a young newlywed.
F. JAY HAYNES, 1904. HAYNES FOUNDATION COLLECTION, MONTANA HISTORICAL SOCIETY RESEARCH CENTER PHOTOGRAPH ARCHIVES, HELENA, MONTANA.

that he'd been closing up the inn for the season one winter night with only one other staff member in the building. While lying in his room, reading, he heard someone running down the hall just outside his door. He looked out into the hall a couple of times but saw nothing. At midnight he left his room and walked to the balcony that overlooks the lobby. That's when he looked up and saw a figure on the stairs. It was there for a few moments, he said, and then it vanished. Later, after moving back to his home in Missoula, Montana, he told a coworker from the inn that he'd discovered a woman had been murdered in the hotel in 1915, in Room 127. She'd been found in the bathtub in her wedding dress, missing her head.

There is no legitimate record of a murder being committed at the Old Faithful Inn in 1915.

Bornemann had been telling the story since 1983, which is when he made up the whole thing. He actually had heard some phantom footsteps in the hallway, he said, and that gave him the idea for the whole horror story, which he cooked up as a way to give the inn some mystique. Like many legends that are repeated through the years, this one has taken on a life of its own.

Several guests who have stayed in Room 127 have reported unusual activity in the room, most commonly waking in the night to see the figure of a woman—head attached—standing at the foot of the bed, wearing a frilly, white, 1800s-style dress. Enthusiasts of the supernatural hypothesize that this could be the ghost of the murdered bride, or possibly the spirit of Mattie Shipley Culver, the wife of the winter keeper of the long-defunct Firehole Hotel, which was located not too far from Old Faithful. She died at age thirty and is buried in the park near the Nez Perce River. Culver died in childbirth, and it's speculated that her spirit wanders the area, heartbroken over the tragedy of not being able to see her child grow up.

Other spirits are said to haunt the grand old inn as well. The ghost of a child, upset over having been separated from his parents, has been reportedly seen a few times on the hotel's mezzanine. The boy, according to the stories, runs up to a stranger, crying and asking whether they've seen his parents, and then he vanishes. No one can explain why he doesn't just check with the front desk.

Some people claim that they've seen the ghost of inn architect Robert Reamer himself, his spirit hanging around to watch people enjoying themselves in his grand hotel.

A hotel employee claims to have witnessed a fire extinguisher swiveling on its mount on a wall of its own accord, turning ninety degrees and then dropping back into position. Guests have seen orbs—balls of light attributed to trans-dimensional spirits—floating across their room at the inn. Doorknobs rattle, footfalls echo down an empty hallway, doors open and close by themselves.

As much as people love a good ghost story, it takes only a cursory examination of the environment to provide plausible explanations for virtually all of these mystery noises. For one thing, this massive log building that was constructed in 1903–1904 sits atop an active volcano, the Yellowstone caldera. Earthquakes, sometimes hundreds in a day, constantly ripple through the area. Most are too small to be felt at the surface, but there's enough activity to cause any number of creaks, pops, groans, and other sounds in a century-old building constructed of stacked logs. In addition, the hotel is still partially heated by old radiators, which are notorious for their spooky noises. On top of all that, the surrounding basin is home to the highest concentration of geysers in the world, many of which are erupting at all hours of the day and night. It's not beyond the realm of possibility that some guests, especially those who are looking for a paranormal thrill, might misinterpret some of the hissing or booming sounds of a geyser as voices from the beyond.

And let's not forget the creatures that live in this dimension. Bull elk, especially in late summer, have a habit of rubbing their massive antlers on the lodgepole pines to help shed the old velvet from the bone. It's quite noisy, and it sends a signal to the other elk that says, "Hear that? No velvet!" Yellowstone's iconic bison also frequent the area, and the snort of an annoyed bull can carry clear across the basin. And then there are the coyotes, which begin yipping and yowling in the nearby hills as the sun goes down. Nature itself provides such a wild cacophony that it would be easy for some guests of the Old Faithful Inn to let their imaginations run amok and attribute these exotic sounds to a preternatural source. There are explanations for virtually every mysterious bump and grind heard in the hotel, but thanks to the infinite redundancy of the internet, the same stale legends keep circulating despite the lack of proof such as a photo, video, or sound recording. Hotel staff are reticent about these ghastly tales, and it's assumed that the management of the Old Faithful Inn would rather not promote the hotel's reputation as a haunted structure for fear of being overrun with gear-wielding ghost hunters and other enthusiasts of the paranormal.

Room 127 has had its share of alleged misfortune, but not all of it was of the paranormal variety. One pair of guests checked into

Room 127 in 2015, and things went badly almost from the get-go. They shared their unpleasant experience on an online travel rating site, and what they found in Room 127 caused them to lose sleep and question their decision to book a room at the historic hotel. Were they terrorized by a ghost or creeped out by some other unexplained phenomena? Nope. Evidently unaware of the room's reputation, they just found their accommodations to be unsatisfactory.

Room 127, they said in their unintentionally hilarious diatribe, was loud. It's situated just behind the hotel bar, which was open until the ungodly hour of 10:00 p.m. Through the log walls of their room, they could hear every conversation and every sound of the staff opening the bar and cleaning up after closing. Outside their room the constant noise of people chattering and laughing on the adjacent balcony was unbearable. People eating, talking, sitting and drinking—the nerve! And the noise of the metal luggage trolleys rattling across the lobby floor! How was a person supposed to sleep? Reading in their room was impossible. These big dark logs used to build the hotel just didn't reflect any light. Even though they requested a lighter lampshade from the front desk, it still proved too dim for reading. They removed the shade and suffered the indignity of a bare bulb. Not only that, but the room also came equipped with only one chair. One chair! For two people! Oh, this Room 127 was indeed a living hell. The guests requested a different room, but the only one available was overlooking a construction site. Their crushing disappointment after making their reservations a year and a half in advance was almost too much to take. The food in the dining room was good, they said, but after bombarding the front desk with complaints and then posting their blistering harangue online, these travelers make one wonder what exactly they were expecting at a century-old rustic lodge. Imagine the zero-star review they might have left if they'd been woken up in the middle of the night by a headless bride standing at the foot of their bed.

While the Old Faithful Inn is the most popular subject of purported hauntings and paranormal activity in the park, it is by no means the only Yellowstone spot to be the focus of apocryphal ghost stories. Next to the headless bride thriller, the next most popular spook yarn is probably the one about the phantom bellman who lurks at the Lake Yellowstone Hotel.

A sighting of the elderly, uniformed hotel employee usually goes like this: The hotel guests, usually a couple, arrive at the hotel after a long day of overland travel or touring the park. They're exhausted. They need a cold drink and a hot shower. Their room is on one of the upper floors, so they head for the elevator. An old bellman wearing a vintage uniform materializes and relieves the guests of their heavy bags and walks them to the elevator (or stairs, depending on the physical fitness of the storyteller). While escorting the guests to their rooms, the friendly bellman shares all kinds of tips and suggestions about how to enjoy the park, where the best hikes are, where to see wildlife, and so on. He sees the guests to their door, but before they can palm him a fiver, he vanishes. Later the guests walk to the dining room for dinner, passing the front desk along the way. They freeze in their tracks as they spot a framed photo of a group of bellmen on the counter. They recognize the face of the kindly old man who helped them earlier. They inquire about the bellman and receive the chilling information that the gentleman in the photo had indeed worked at the hotel, but he's been dead for years.

Boo.

When you're talking about a venerable national park that's as rife with history as Yellowstone, tall tales and ghost stories just come with the territory. Add to the mix the variety of unfortunate deaths that have occurred in the park, whether at the hand of man or from the random whims of nature, and it's a breeding ground for embellishment. But why perpetrate the fiction? The actual history of the park is bursting with amazing tales of adventure, larger-than-life characters, and enough real drama to fuel hundreds of fascinating *true* stories. Ghost stories can provide some great campfire fun and even tidbits of real history here and there, but these persistent legends of hauntings and spirits should be taken with a grain of salt. Hey, this is Yellowstone. Better use the whole shaker.

CHAPTER 7

The Zone of Death

So there's that one person you just don't think deserves to take up space on this planet any longer. You want them gone. Taken off the board. Disappeared. You could go the normal route and poison their Lucky Charms, drop a piano on their head, or have them pose a little too close to the edge while taking a photo at the Grand Canyon. You could even hire someone who specializes in this sort of thing if you don't want to get your hands dirty. Unfortunately for your homicidal impulses, these avenues all run the risk of detection. Even if you try to make it look like an accident, today's advanced forensic sciences, using techniques like microspectrophotometry and drone-assisted 3-D computer modeling, leave little hope for you to commit the crime and not do the time. But what if there were a place where you could kill someone in cold blood, right out in the open, and be immune from the threat of Johnny Law? Well, guess what—Yellowstone Park might offer just the situation you're looking for.

There's a fifty-square-mile sliver of wilderness where Yellowstone extends into the eastern edge of Idaho. A loophole in the law created a unique legal situation in which a person could commit a murder in this part of the park but never be brought to trial for the crime. Does the Zone of Death actually exist? How did it come to be? And has anyone ever put it to the test?

With his wife two weeks away from giving birth to their first child in 2004, Brian C. Kalt, a law professor at Michigan State University, was scrambling to finish a paper when he discovered an interesting gray area. When creating our first national park in 1872, Congress placed the entire park in Wyoming's federal district, including the 9 percent of the park that slopped over into Montana and Idaho. This was nearly twenty years before those states were admitted to the Union, but the territories ceded their narrow swaths of land that overlapped the park to the Wyoming district. As with all national parks, Yellowstone is federal land, including the areas that lie within Idaho and Montana. Article III of the US Constitution states that if someone commits a federal crime (which would be any felony committed on federal land), they are required to be tried in the venue, or state, where the crime was committed. So far, no big deal. Kalt also knew that the Sixth Amendment gives a federal criminal defendant the right to a trial by jury in which the jurors are chosen from the state and district where the deed was done. This jury source is known as vicinage. Here's where the black and white blurs to gray: In the uninhabited chunk of Idaho wilderness that lies within Yellowstone's western perimeter, it would be impossible to seat a jury. No one lives there. In all of the United States, this is the only spot Kalt could find where this situation exists. Federal crimes committed in the Idaho portion of Yellowstone would be in the state of Idaho, but also in the federal District of Wyoming. It's a catch-22 of constitutional venue and vicinage.

Once he discovered the Zone of Death situation, Kalt quickly wrapped up his fourteen-page paper and submitted it to the *Georgetown Law Journal*. It was scheduled for publication the following year. Kalt, however, was worried that some nefarious type might stumble upon the jurisdictional get-out-of-jail-free card and carry out an actual murder in the remote forest of Yellowstone's southwest corner. He quickly devised a simple fix for Congress to close the loophole and sent it—along with copies of his paper—to the Department of Justice, the US attorney in Wyoming, and the House and Senate judiciary committees. Thank heavens he'd acted in time, he thought. Now Congress could act swiftly to repair the discrepancy and avert potential calamity in Yellowstone Park.

The silence of Congress's response was deafening. They couldn't have cared less about the situation and didn't make any moves to correct it. "If Congress really wanted to fix this," said Kalt in a 2016 interview, "it wouldn't take long at all. The problem isn't that it's complicated; it's that they're not interested in it."

When his paper was published in 2005 with the title "The Perfect Crime," suddenly the issue got loads of attention. Not from Congress, though—from the media. His article received coverage from the *Washington Post*, NPR, BBC, even a Japanese newspaper. The story also caught the eye of Wyoming novelist C. J. Box, whose books regularly land on the *New York Times* bestseller list. Box made several visits to Yellowstone, making the Old Faithful Inn his base of operations while he researched and wrote *Free Fire*, the seventh book in his Joe Pickett series. In the book, his Wyoming Game and Fish warden protagonist is pitted against a West Yellowstone lawyer who shoots four campers in cold blood in the Zone of Death. Well aware of the jurisdictional problems with the area, the lawyer calmly walks out of the forest and turns himself in to a wide-eyed ranger at the park's tiny Bechler ranger station, surrendering the still-warm murder weapon and confessing to the crime. *Free Fire* was published in 2008 and vaulted to the #1 spot on the bestseller list. Sales of the book are still steady at every Yellowstone gift shop that stocks it.

Surely there must be some legal maneuvering that could circumvent this constitutional goof. Couldn't a federal court in a capital murder trial find a way around this antiquated legal conundrum? Well, it's a complex situation. If a felony is committed in the Idaho portion of Yellowstone, the crime cannot technically be charged as a federal crime, even though all national parks are considered federal land. Yellowstone is the only national park that incorporates more than one state. The Act of Dedication in 1872 did not include Idaho as part of Yellowstone, but when the District Court of Wyoming was created, legislators drew the district line to include all of Yellowstone Park, including those bits of Idaho and Montana it overlaps. They inadvertently created a legal no-man's land. Crime in the Yellowstone area, such as poaching game and vandalizing the park's features, was rampant and going unpunished, so, before sending the US Army in to restore order, instead of creating three districts, Congress took the path of least resistance and included those chunks of Montana and Idaho. When their statehoods were achieved in 1889 and 1890, respectively, it must have seemed more important at the time to maintain Wyoming's sleek trapezoid shape than to redraw the boundaries and include that 9 percent of

Yellowstone that lay in the adjoining states. That's when Congress really stepped in it, creating a situation where a rather large legal technicality could potentially free a murderer.

Article III, sec. 2 states that the trial must be held in the state where the crime was committed and—this is the important part—must be a jury trial. With the Sixth Amendment specifying that the trial also must be held in the district where the crime was committed, there's your rub. All the US states have their own district court that includes the entire state—except Idaho and Montana, which, remember, allowed those Yellowstone parts of their states to be included in Wyoming's district. It's a sticky wicket.

The problem of venue versus vicinage isn't a new one. In his paper Professor Kalt points out that in England, before 1548, a murderer would "strike his victim" in one county and make sure they died in another, making it impossible to seat a jury for a trial, since the victim perished outside the perpetrator's own county, where the initial crime was committed. In the United States, Article III was drafted to address the problem, which frequently occurred when British soldiers who'd killed colonists were brought back to England for trial.

A similar situation cropped up in the United States in 1888, when a band of murderers killed four people in the Oklahoma panhandle. At the time, that little square of land didn't actually belong to any state. The killers figured that since their crime didn't occur in any state, they couldn't be prosecuted. After the murder, Congress assigned the panhandle to the Eastern District of Texas. The killers protested that this trampled their rights by violating Article III and the Sixth Amendment. In *Cook v. United States*, the US Supreme Court rejected their argument, stating that if a crime is not in any state, then the remainder of Article III provides that "[t]he Trial shall be at such Place or Places as the Congress may by Law have directed." Since Article III refers explicitly to a state, Kalt wrote, the Sixth Amendment takes a backseat to Article III.

It could be argued that if you commit a felony in the Zone of Death, you're on federal land and not really in Idaho. This isn't true. In the sliver of Idaho that resides within the Wyoming district, residents (if there were any) would vote in Idaho elections, pay Idaho taxes, register their vehicles with Idaho, and so forth. The same holds true for the Montana section of Yellowstone Park. So while these overlapped sections of land belong to their respective states, they also belong to the *district* of Wyoming.

Since no one lives in that section of Idaho/Wyoming/Yellowstone, there's no pool from which to draw a local jury. No jury, no trial. Case dismissed! But what about a bench trial? Then a jury wouldn't have to be seated, solving the issue of the nonexistent Idaho population in the Zone of Death. Here the law comes down on the rights of the accused. The defendant would have to waive his right to a jury trial. And who's going to do that when he has a shot at the perfect crime? Professor Kalt addressed this question in an online fact-checking site in 2016: "The defendant also cannot be forced to have a bench trial. He can assert his right to a jury trial—there cannot be a bench trial without the defendant waiving that right. Similarly, he can assert his right to a local jury. Only he can waive that. There is precedent supporting the notion that if the defendant cannot be given a proper jury, and he refuses to waive his rights, then the charges must be dismissed."

Looking across the Bechler River toward Bechler Meadows in the so-called Zone of Death.

EDNOR THERRIAULT.

Outside the fictional world of a novel, how hard would it actually be to pull off a capital crime in the Zone of Death? Even if it's technically possible to get away with murder, there are several factors that make the idea a pretty far-fetched scenario in real life. For one thing, the crime would have to be spontaneous and happen entirely within the prescribed area of park. Any planning, like gearing up with shovels and duct tape or hashing over your scheme with some friends, is called conspiracy to commit murder and shows premeditation. You might also commit some federal firearms violation, or any number of lesser crimes that could trip you up. You'd be committing those lesser crimes in states and districts that have no venue/vicinage issue if they weren't felonies. If you pull off your murder but wind up getting charged with, say, misdemeanor manslaughter (which is a murder committed during the commission of a non-felony crime), the State of Idaho could get involved. Any lesser offense than a felony that could result in jail time of six months or less wouldn't require a jury trial. These crimes could be prosecuted with the full force of whatever state or district in which they're committed.

An even bigger obstacle to committing the perfect murder is one of logistics. We're talking about a remote piece of country here, an area that's not even connected by roads to the rest of Yellowstone. You have to leave the park and drive to Ashton, Idaho, where you take a ten-mile dirt road back into the park. If you are going to the Zone of Death by way of the south entrance of the park, you pick up Grassy Lake Road, which heads west to Ashton-Flagg Ranch Road and runs perpendicular to the park's southern border for forty miles of bone-jarring, teeth-rattling, eyeball-jiggling, low-gear dirt road full of ruts, rocks, washboards, and whoop-de-dos. The scenery is gorgeous—if you can manage to focus your eyes. It takes about three hours, so make sure you have a full tank of gas and a spare tire.

Once you've passed the Bechler ranger station and reached the Bechler Meadows trailhead, you have to convince your intended victim to hike up through the woods along the Bechler River. You could entice them with promised views of the Bechler Falls or the incredible trout fishing to be had at the little-visited Bechler Meadows, but they might not hear you over the whine of thousands of monster mosquitoes that inhabit the area, waiting for their next warm-blooded meal. Seriously, if you want to survive long enough to make sure that you walk back alone, a DEET bath would be advisable.

And even if you're able to lure your unsuspecting victim into the Zone of Death and administer the coup de grace, you'll be faced with a number of natural hazards that still stand between you and freedom. The Caribou-Targhee Forest is a favorite haunt of grizzlies and wolves. If you can't get in and out before sundown, well, you might wind up doubling the workload of some search party long after you and your quarry have been reported missing.

And let's not forget the specter of a civil lawsuit. If you're somehow able to avoid prosecution through application of the Zone of Death's constitutional square knot, you might still get the pants sued off you by the family of the gullible rube you lured into the woods.

It just doesn't seem worth the trouble.

For the sake of argument, let's say a killer was determined enough to overcome all these obstacles and commit a capital crime. Wouldn't that command the attention of Congress long enough to apply a legislative fix? The short answer: nope. Kalt wrote, "Congress cannot change the district after the crime. The Previous Ascertainment Clause ties to the time of the crime, not the time of the trial. The point is to prevent the government from manipulating district lines to disadvantage the defendant, which is exactly what they would be doing if they changed it after the fact (especially since they have had ample opportunity to redraw the district lines before the crime occurred)."

The Sixth Amendment exists largely to keep the prosecution or defense in a trial from jury-shopping. It's a clear-cut element of the Constitution, but the main issue that creates the problem, said Kalt, is the sloppy drawing of the districts to begin with. If the constitutional framers had only taken the time to create three districts, giving those small portions to the states they cover instead of just pulling it all into Wyoming, this boondoggle wouldn't exist. As it stands, while there may be some way for Congress to propose legislation that would eliminate the Zone of Death scenario, they just aren't interested in the issue of vicinage, and even less so in spending the time on undoing a nineteenth-century goof that created this obscure constitutional mess.

Of course, we don't condone or endorse the commission of murder in Yellowstone Park. The thought of homicide occurring within the boundaries of this national gem runs counter to its phenomenal natural splendor. Still, murder happens, both in Yellowstone and in other national parks. In July 2013 newlywed Jordan Linn Graham pushed her husband Cody Johnson off the edge of a cliff along Going-to-the-Sun Road in Glacier National Park. With no Zone of Death protection, she confessed a week later to the FBI.

Yosemite National Park was terrorized in 1999 when four women were murdered by Cary Anthony Stayner, a handyman at a motel just outside the park. His first two victims were found stuffed into the trunk of their car, burned beyond recognition. A crude note from him to the FBI led them to a third victim, the daughter of one of the initial pair, a week later. Stayner, who worked at the motel where they'd been staying, was interviewed and released. That summer the decapitated body of a young park naturalist was found in Yosemite, and evidence led investigators back to Stayner. He is still on death row in California.

James Lee Hamar was traveling through Yellowstone with a companion in 1978. The two boys, both seventeen, were either swimming or getting ready to swim in the Boiling River near Mammoth Hot Springs when they got into an altercation. Hamar was shot in the back by his friend and later died at the Mammoth clinic. The shooter was remanded to Cheyenne and charged with murder.

Killings in Yellowstone were not uncommon in the late 1800s when the park was under the rule of the US Army, which was based at Fort Yellowstone near Mammoth. They had only a handful of men to patrol the 2.2 million acres of the park, and lawless behavior was the order of the day. There are several documented murders among trappers and other men who came into the park to poach its resources, but one of the most gruesome killings was at the hands of the wife of an army carpenter at Fort Yellowstone. As detailed in chapter 5, George Trischman had brought his wife, Margaret, home to Mammoth from the state mental asylum in Warm Springs, Montana, in 1899, and a few days later she slashed the throat of her own five-year-old son, nearly severing his head. For her crime, she was shipped off to the federal asylum in Washington, DC. She never made it. It's believed that she jumped off the train somewhere in the Paradise Valley. No trace of her was ever found.

Nowadays, with more than four million visitors pouring into Yellowstone each year, it's accidental deaths and injuries that get the headlines. Deliberate killings at the hands of humans are few and far between. However, until Congress decides to do something about the jurisdictional glitch that has created the Zone of Death, there's a remote corner of Yellowstone Park where—as far as the Constitution is concerned—you can indeed get away with murder.

CHAPTER 8

Bigfoot in Yellowstone?

hristmas Day 2014. While countless people around the world opened gifts, assembled toys, and argued about who was supposed to make the coffee, an astonishing scene was apparently being captured on a National Park Service (NPS) webcam at Old Faithful in Yellowstone National Park. In the video, clouds of steam drift through the air on an otherwise clear, sunny winter day. Four shaggy bison mosey through the snow in a desultory search for food. After a couple of minutes of this bucolic scene, a figure emerges in the clearing between the snow-clotted pine trees behind the bison. A black humanoid shape strides across the snow, followed by three other figures walking in single file. The creatures disappear behind a tree, closing on the oblivious bison. One walks into view past the tree, and . . . the video ends.

The video was posted four days later on YouTube by someone named Mary Greeley. The internet went nuts. To date there are almost two million views. Was this Bigfoot? Holy cryptid, was this a *family* of Bigfoots? Hunting bison on Christmas Day? In Yellowstone Park? It was all just so much to take in. But why not? Yellowstone is situated just a state away from Washington, which boasts more Bigfoot sightings than anywhere else in North America. But Yellowstone is also home to many large mammals, including bears and moose. Bears have been known to stand on their hind legs, with some grizzlies reaching a height of ten feet. But these beasts following the bison were no bears. The video clearly shows four tall, dark, human-like beings walking across the snow, swinging their arms and striding purposefully as if they're trying to get to the Old Faithful gift shop before closing time. At long last, was this the irrefutable evidence that would prove once and for all that the elusive Bigfoot really exists?

Nearly every culture across the earth has its traditional stories of a mysterious, hairy, ape-like giant who lives just out of sight of people. Sasquatch, Yeti, Skunk Ape, Myakka Ape, Yeren, Yowie—some version of Bigfoot has been reportedly spotted on every continent except Antarctica. In North America, sightings of an unidentified bipedal hominid or what appear to be its giant footprints have been reported for at least two hundred years. The earliest North American report on record may be that of famed British Canadian trader David Thompson, who explored and mapped much of North America. In 1811, near what now is the town of Jasper, Alberta, Canada, Thompson found some strange footprints in the snow that measured fourteen inches long and eight inches wide. Each footprint had four toes.

In the early 1970s, Sasquatch blew up. The number of sightings skyrocketed, especially in the Pacific Northwest, and Bigfoot became a ubiquitous cultural phenomenon. Even the National Park Service got in on the act, funding a field study seeking Bigfoot evidence. They found diddly squat.

The celebrated Patterson-Gimlin footage of a purported Bigfoot shot in Northern California in 1967 remains the gold standard of Bigfoot "evidence." The famous shot of Patty (as the subject is known in Bigfoot circles) looking back over her shoulder toward the camera has become a cultural icon. The pose has been aped in hundreds of parodies, perhaps most famously by Will Farrell in the movie *Elf.* Debates have raged for fifty years over the authenticity of the ten-second film, but no one has come forward to confess to a hoax, nor has science been able to conclusively debunk it. Roger Patterson, who shot the footage, took the truth with him to his grave in 1972. Bob Gimlin, sick of the notoriety—both positive and negative—had washed his hands of the sensational film, but in the last decade he has resurfaced, having made his peace with his role in capturing the legendary footage. Now he attends Bigfoot conferences, where he is greeted as a rock star, signing autographs, posing for photos, and recounting the story of the famous expedition that produced the clip. He maintains that the film is the real deal.

But is it? Could an entire species of giant hominids live, breed, and thrive while avoiding human detection? After all, there's never been a corpse or body part found (Sasquatch families quickly bury their dead, claim Bigfoot enthusiasts). Supposed Bigfoot hair and scat samples have been DNA tested but have invariably been identified as bear, elk, possum, or even human (those tests are faulty, say cryptozoologists; we need to find the right geneticist). Photos or videos that claim to show the creature are notoriously blurry or partially obscured (if only we'd remembered to remove the lens cap . . .). Especially in this day and age, when surveillance cameras are everywhere and most of us carry a camera phone, it's kind of amazing that the internet isn't flooded with endless videos and still shots of the mystery creature.

The Bigfoot Field Research Organization, the oldest and largest group of its type, maintains an exhaustive list of sightings and encounters on its website. Such accounts occurring in Yellowstone Park are scant. The most recent report is from 2002, when a family of four driving along the northwest side of Mount Washburn "saw a humanoid figure, too tall to be human, walking upright along a ridge around 300 yards off." It was noon, under cloudy skies, and the family had been scanning the ridge for bighorn sheep. The BFRO had one of its investigators interview the family by phone, and he dutifully posted his findings on the BFRO website:

> As they drove north along Grand Loop Road in the vicinity of Mount Washburn in Yellowstone National Park, they observed a dark bipedal animal silhouetted on a ridge about 300 to 400 yards from them walking purposefully across a clearing between stands of trees. The animal's direction of movement was southerly. The biped was described by all as being about eight to nine feet tall, covered with dark brown hair, having a robust upper body with a large, wide chest and shoulders and walking upslope much as human would—slightly bent forward as a person might be if they were using a walking stick. Arm swing was implied.

It's been noted in much of the Sasquatch research that their quarry's preferred habitat is identical to that of the American black bear, an animal that is frequently misidentified as a Bigfoot. This 2002 Yellowstone sighting, though, seems to rule out the black bear. "The witness' mother stated that she looked for a snout, but saw none although the animal was in profile. All three [witnesses] were consistent in their recollection of the sighting and are considered to be credible."

Credibility—and its subsequent loss—is one of the main reasons you don't hear about Bigfoot in Yellowstone Park. Tom Brodhead, a BFRO investigator from Livingston, Montana, understands the reticence:

> There's a lot of stories out there, you just have to dig 'em out. You have to be attuned to it. I hear stories, and it's just anecdotal, you have to take it for what it's worth. The backcountry guides have had a number of sightings but they won't talk to anybody about it. They're under the impression that people would think they're nuts. If you could get the rangers to talk [about Bigfoot sightings], but they never do. Very rarely do you get a ranger. You may get some of the old timers who are close to retirement or something. I think they're afraid for their jobs.

He recalls a female ranger who kept a journal of Bigfoot sightings, a frowned-upon practice in the park. Upon her death, the book, with thirty years' worth of Bigfoot sightings, mysteriously disappeared from her station.

Brodhead, who runs a successful company that manufactures fly lines in Montana, is "99% sure" that Bigfoot is out there. He dismisses the idea that people who claim to have seen the creature are all crackpots or attention seekers:

> After dealing with people for a while you get a pretty good feel for if somebody's giving a line or if somebody's sincere. A lot of people, they're really sincere people. They're not looking to make money off it, they're not looking to get on YouTube. They're just like, "I just wanted to tell my story." There are reputable people like Dr. Meldrum at Idaho State. He's a physical anthropologist and he studies footprint morphology so he's pretty up on it. I think he's convinced that there's something out there.

Dr. Jeff Meldrum actually stops short of saying he's a true believer. "Besides having grown up in the Pacific Northwest and being aware of the history and so forth, my professional interest in the subject stands from the tangent that the prospect of another bipedal upright primate in our own backyard is an intriguing one, and a very interesting natural experiment to shed light on our own adaptation." He does indeed specialize in footprint morphology—more specifically, primate adaptations to walking on two legs, the emergence of human bipedalism. The question of the existence of a whole new biological species behind the folklore is an appropriate one to address from a scientific perspective, he feels. Like Brodhead, he understands the general hesitancy of people to share their experiences when they think they've seen a Bigfoot in Yellowstone. An acquaintance of Meldrum's is working on an oral history project with tribal members on the Wind River Reservation in Wyoming, which lies within the Greater Yellowstone Ecosystem. As he gains the trust of the tribal elders, he's starting to hear more and more stories of encounters with a large, hairy ape-man that go back hundreds of years. The stories are passed down to each generation and rarely told outside the family. Many encounters took place in what is now Yellowstone Park.

Meldrum has an impressive collection of purported Sasquatch footprint casts, one of the largest in the world. He's an occasional speaker at Bigfoot conferences and a well-known name in cryptozoology circles. Still, his interest in the existence of the elusive hominid is a dispassionate one based in science. To that end, he has an agreement with a professional tracker he knows in Gardiner, Montana (at the north entrance to the park), a PhD wildlife biologist who specializes in large carnivores like bears and wolves and frequently leads field trips into Yellowstone Park. "He's given me the open standing challenge that as soon as I find a good trackline [of Bigfoot prints], just give him a call and wherever it is he'll come and he said we'll track it out together and get to the bottom of it."

The application of scientific methodology in the search for bipedal cryptids is particularly difficult, Meldrum points out, because of the various motivations behind the encounters. This includes deliberate hoaxes:

For me, individuals like that cross the line when it becomes intellectual sabotage. The novelty of [Bigfoot] is long past and so everyone now looks askance at anything. And you have to because that's one of the problems of trying to conduct serious science in this arena. In other areas, you don't really have that initial challenge of winnowing through all of the pranks. It's one thing when I have to deal with misidentifications when it comes to footprints with over-enthusiastic and highly suggestible amateur investigators. Everything that has even the vaguest resemblance to a footprint then takes on a new aura of mystique and I have to deal with that.

Having to discern between the real and the fake muddies the waters even further. The constant flow of Bigfoot hoaxes that are posted to the internet, including the infamous Christmas Day Old Faithful video—which has been thoroughly debunked, by the way—make Meldrum's research that much harder.

So, other than the occasional doctored footage, why haven't we heard much about any Bigfoot activity in Yellowstone? Perhaps the lack of reporting doesn't necessarily indicate a lack of encounters. When you think about the richest resource of information about strange animal activity in the park, you'd probably want to hear from the people who spend the most time out in it. And who spends more time covering more territory in Yellowstone than its park rangers? Surely, if anyone has seen a Sasquatch with their own two eyes, it's a ranger. But, as Tom Brodhead pointed out, they're not talking. Well, most of them aren't.

Known as the "Bigfoot hotspot," this section of US Highway 14 approaching the east entrance to Yellowstone has produced many reports of Bigfoot sightings. Sascha Burkard © 123RF.com.

Bob Jackson, also known as "Action Jackson," was the last of his breed. The Yellowstone ranger spent thirty years patrolling the park's remote backcountry, including the Thorofare, a remote section of wilderness that sprawls across the southeast corner. Jackson specialized in nailing poachers, and he had a particular disdain for outfitters and hunters who used salt licks to lure their prey near the park boundaries. Frequently the gut piles and carcasses of elk were left to rot after being shot near these bait spots, which would attract grizzlies from their protected sanctuary in the park. Bears were being needlessly killed, and Jackson complained long and loud not only to his superiors in the National Park Service but also to the press. His penchant for speaking his mind to the media earned him the enmity of many an outfitter, and he was eventually slapped with a gag order from his NPS bosses. In 2004 his contract was not renewed and he was forced to retire. Conservation groups loved him, poachers feared him, outfitters hated him, and journalists always knew he was good for a juicy quote. His firing after three decades in the Park Service was officially attributed to his job performance, but beyond that the park administration was pretty tight-lipped. Jackson became a legendary figure in Yellowstone, one of the most colorful rangers to ever wear the uniform. One thing that was never called into question was Bob Jackson's integrity.

Shortly before he left the park in 2004 to return to his native Iowa to raise bison, Action Jackson granted an interview with T. E. Stein of the Bigfoot Field Research Organization. For the first time, he shared publicly his story of encountering strange creatures in Yellowstone Park. He'd been hiking in the late 1970s near Fan

Creek, he recalled, in the northwest corner of the park. He heard a howling sound coming from the Stellaria Creek drainage, about a mile away. "It filled the whole valley up," he said. "Kind of like a thousand elk going to their death." Jackson said he and the outfitter he was traveling with had never heard a sound like that in the backcountry. A couple of weeks later, he had another run-in with an unidentified creature in the same area. He was riding his horse down into a flat meadow dotted with stubby fir trees, each surrounded by a cone of smaller bushes. He estimated that these tree "islands" were about twenty feet wide.

"The horses were flaring their noses and snorting, like they do when a grizzly bear is real close, but I could see fairly good all around and I couldn't see one," he said. Looking down into the meadow, he didn't see any bear. He did see a deer at the edge of a thicket, and when the deer bolted he saw something come running out of the trees. "It was like a black bear and it had long arms and ran." Then he noticed some very non-bearlike behavior when the creature started darting between the clusters of trees. "It kept hitting these thickets trying to get away from me. I've never seen a bear do that. They'll always take a straight line." He remembered the spine-tingling cry he'd heard a couple of weeks earlier. "I realized this black shaggy thing wasn't a bear. The side of the face looked like it had a lot of fur. Most of the time it was angling away, so I only got a good look at the head for probably the first ten steps."

After that experience Jackson started asking around, wondering whether anyone else had heard these weird noises out in the backcountry or seen this bipedal creature running around. He heard a few stories, he recalled, and the common element was the loud, protracted howl that sounded like nothing he'd ever heard. "I can't even describe it. It isn't like a mountain lion or bear, and bear can make some pretty weird noises.

"I've ridden maybe fifty thousand to seventy thousand miles in the backcountry. This was no hoax."

Was Jackson's story the concoction of a disgruntled employee who saw the writing on the wall and wanted to create some PR heartburn for his soon-to-be ex-employer? Or was it the case of a man unburdening himself of a secret he'd carried around for more than twenty-five years, unsure whether he could even believe what he'd seen and heard? Without hard evidence like a photo or a tissue sample of the creature, or even a body, it's impossible to know for sure.

"Bigfoot sightings [in the park] are not frequent, but it happens," said Yellowstone spokesman Al Nash in an interview. "People say a lot of crazy things about Yellowstone all the time and Bigfoot is just one of them." The park's official line may be to disavow any knowledge of Bigfoot, but that doesn't stop them from letting the search go on. In 2014 the NPS green-lighted a permit for a film crew to spend ten weeks in the park hunting for the creature, shooting footage for an Adventure Channel TV reality show. Park spokesman Stan Thatch told *Yellowstone Gate*, "So long as production doesn't interfere with normal park operations and abides by the terms and conditions of the permit, they will be allowed to tape segments about Bigfoot—or any other-sized-foot animals they might find here."

Although such a program would generate extra publicity for the park and ultimately contribute to the economy of the gateway towns, some critics were concerned about the message inherent in such a venture. "This flies in the face of the educational and interpretive mission the Park Service is supposed to be carrying out," said Sharm Dresden, wildlife policy specialist for the Friends of Yellowstone Alliance. "We wouldn't allow a crew to film a 'Leprechaun Search' show at the Lincoln Memorial, so why is this being permitted?"

Thatch, tongue planted firmly in cheek, added, "We do track things like reports of wolves with sarcoptic mange, for instance. Our biologists want to stay on top of that. But there is no crypto-zoologist on staff at Yellowstone, so we don't keep up with Yetis, dragons, or mermaids."

Some days are probably more fun than others when you're a national park spokesperson.

BFRO's website is rife with breathless reports of sightings near the park, most notably in the "Bigfoot hotspot" along the section of US Highway 14, a two-lane blacktop that runs fifty-two miles between Cody, Wyoming, and the park's east entrance. Eyewitness accounts describe run-ins with the creature day and night, by people who were out cutting firewood, hiking, or simply cruising along on their way to Yellowstone. But once they get into the park, Bigfoot activity flatlines. Yellowstone's a big place, and although it's visited by millions of people every year, vast areas of the park are rarely seen by human eyes. But are there some other eyes out there watching, waiting, lurking in the woods? If so, why are they so hard to find?

According to Tom Brodhead,

The thing is, you can't really go out looking for these guys, you know, you see people wearing camouflage and they're being quiet, but if they're what they claim to be, they know you're there. I'll go out and just kind of walk around a little bit and do some talking and come back to camp. And then things start happening around camp. That's really what you can do, basically just hope that their sense of curiosity will bring them back to you. And it happens more often than not, they'll follow you back to camp.

Thus far there has been no irrefutable evidence that proves the existence of Bigfoot, in Yellowstone National Park or anywhere else. But that won't keep the faithful from searching. They're out there, the Bigfoot hunters, hoping to bring home that missing piece of the puzzle—a photo, a video, maybe even a Sasquatch carcass—to prove once and for all that a previously unknown species of primate does indeed exist.

CHAPTER 9

How One Arrest Saved Yellowstone's Buffalo

The huge, woolly beast brushes the bumper of your car as it lumbers casually past. Its deep, guttural snort sounds like the exhaust of a Chevy pickup. There are dozens of buffalo making their way en masse from one side of the road to the other, and they seem to be in no particular hurry to do so. Their rough, shaggy brown fur is missing in large patches, revealing a sleek hide that covers impressive musculature. They might look ungainly, with their massive heads and tall, narrow bodies that taper down to a skinny rear end, but this king of the Yellowstone beasts can reach speeds of forty-five miles per hour, which, perhaps not coincidentally, is the speed limit throughout the park.

But wait a second—are they buffalo, or are they bison? It's the perennial question, fielded thousands of times by hundreds of guides, rangers, and other workers at Yellowstone. Technically, it is the American bison (*Bison bison*). The only true buffalo in the world are the African buffalo and the Asian water buffalo. The chances of specimens of either of those critters wandering out of their habitat and making their way into Yellowstone Park are pretty slim. Use of the term *buffalo* for the American bison, however, has been generally accepted, even showing up in a few dictionaries.

For the purpose of this book, let's say that "buffalo" is the animals' nickname and "bison" the proper handle.

As we learned in our high school history class, millions of bison covered the western plains up until the mid-1800s. They were an essential resource for the indigenous peoples who inhabited North America long before the continent's "discovery" by European explorers. Indians hunted bison with spears on foot or from horseback or by driving them off cliffs known as buffalo jumps, where the animals would be impaled on stakes at the bottom or finished off by sentries waiting to make sure none survived. (They'd learned that bison who did survive the drop became wise to their scheme and could no longer be herded to the cliffs.)

The buffalo were sacred animals to the Indians, who believed that they were provided by the Creator to give them a source of clothing, food, tools, and weapons. Tatanka (as the buffalo was known by the Lakota, the tribe with which the animal is most closely associated) was an integral part of the Indians who comprised the Buffalo Nation. The animal's role in the spiritual as well as corporeal sense was so intertwined that there was little distinction between where the lives of the buffalo and those of the Indians diverged.

Then the white man came. The establishment of the transcontinental railroad, coupled with the Homestead Act of 1862, beckoned gold miners, pioneers, trappers, and other adventurous types to fulfill the westward expansion movement spurred by the Louisiana Purchase. "Go West, young man," Horace Greeley's famous phrase, was on everyone's lips.

While Manifest Destiny drove so many people and their dreams out West, it nearly led to the demise of the animal that would eventually become our national mammal. Estimates of the bison population in North America between 1600 and 1870 run as high as several hundred million. Indeed, hundreds of thousands could be seen in a single mass as they thundered across the grassland prairie, shaking the ground beneath their hooves. Herds were reported stretching as long as sixty miles. The railroad—and the advent of the rifle—provided a virtual shooting gallery, as hunters and thrill killers brought their high-powered weapons to bear, shooting from the trains and spreading out into the buffalo's territory to wipe out millions of animals. Most were killing just to kill, although trainloads of buffalo hides and heads were shipped back East, where they would fetch a handsome price. Old photos show the wanton destruction of nearly an entire species, some images featuring a couple of mustachioed men posing proudly next to a mountain of bison skulls as big as a McDonald's.

Today, as the mellow herd of bison surrounds your car during this "traffic jam" in the Lamar Valley, you can usually spot another large herd or two straddling the river across the valley. It's hard to imagine now, but the population of bison in Yellowstone Park, the last stronghold of wild bison in the world, dropped as low as twenty-five animals in 1902. Were it not for the timely apprehension of Yellowstone's most notorious poacher in the winter of 1894, caught literally red-handed while skinning four freshly killed bison, the population might have been snuffed out before the dawn of the twentieth century. Instead of being stopped on Yellowstone's

Grand Loop Road, you would probably be in Cooke City by now, having never had this up-close-and-personal encounter with one of the most magnificent and fascinating creatures to roam the expansive territory of Yellowstone Park.

Yellowstone in winter is a forbidding landscape, with temperatures routinely dropping far below zero and more than twenty feet of snow piling up in some areas. After its official designation as the first national park in 1872, the only people to enter its boundaries in the winter were a few fearless adventurers and hunters looking to bag the elk, antelope, and bison that concentrated in a few areas of the park. There was no real penalty for poaching, which led to a free-for-all of opportunistic mountain men blasting bison with abandon, methodically decimating the winter herds so they could deliver tongues and hides to taxidermists in Bozeman and Livingston, where the price went up as the bison population went down. Elk, antelope, and other animals that wintered in the park were also in their crosshairs. In a two-year period from 1874 to 1875, one pair of particularly prolific hunters, the Bottler brothers, reportedly killed four thousand elk.

In 1875 George Grinnell, a prominent conservationist who ran a magazine called *Forest and Stream*, witnessed firsthand some of this ongoing slaughter in Yellowstone Park and began lobbying the federal government to take action. With bison numbers dwindling, Secretary of the Interior Carl Schurz declared hunting within the park off limits, but enforcing the law would prove difficult. In 1886 the US Army set up a camp near Mammoth Hot Springs and took control of the park. In winter they had exactly one scout to patrol Yellowstone Park's 3,472 square miles—an impossible task. The poaching went on unabated.

Grinnell was becoming alarmed at reports of the shrinking number of bison at their stronghold in Yellowstone Park and sent a man to investigate.

Emerson Hough got off the train in March 1894 at Cinnabar, a small, rambunctious town at the terminus of a spur of the Northern Pacific Railroad. It lay at the foot of Paradise Valley, just a few miles north of Mammoth Hot Springs. Hough was a regular contributor to *Forest and Stream*, and Grinnell had tasked him with performing a firsthand count of the bison in Yellowstone Park. Not a simple job, especially in the brutal environment of a Wyoming winter. The writer wisely employed the assistance of Elwood "Billy" Hofer, a legendary guide who knew the park inside out, winter and summer. Hofer had arrived in Yellowstone in 1877. He wound up staying for fifty years.

Hofer and Hough traveled via mule-drawn buckboard up the hill to Mammoth, where Hough met the acting park superintendent, Captain George Anderson. The fellow sportsmen hit it off immediately, both sharing a love of the outdoors as well as a concern for protecting Yellowstone's big game.

On his way to Cinnabar, Hough had interviewed several taxidermists in Livingston and Bozeman. With a bison carcass bringing as much as $2,000, someone had to be processing the buffalo hides, heads, tongues, and bones and shipping them back East. According to Hough's account of his adventure, every single taxidermist he talked to expressed righteous indignation at the very idea that they would be part of processing an illegally bagged animal, and of course they had never received an ill-gotten bison from a poacher. Somehow, though, the bison were being slaughtered, and their ongoing existence was in jeopardy.

As Hough prepared for his game-counting quest through the park, a series of events was about to unfold that would ultimately lead to the salvation of a species that was hanging by a thread.

Hough's account of his two-month experience in the park was published in an extraordinary fourteen-part series in *Forest and Stream*. The telephone had reached Yellowstone, and the army post was connected (albeit by a glitchy and vulnerable series of lines) to the handful of hotels in the park. This made it possible for the lone scout, Felix Burgess, to report in as he traveled through the park all winter, and it also allowed the keepers at the far-flung hotels a measure of human contact in an otherwise desolate winter existence. Hough used the telephone to file his stories with the *Forest and Stream* office in New York City. The nascent phone system would prove a crucial element in the story, as Hough was able to immediately report poacher Ed Howell's capture to the world at large.

Although snowshoes were available, Hofer made it clear that the preferred method of travel was on skis. These weren't the sleek, high-tech skinny skis that we use today for telemarking or touring the countryside. These were primitive, heavy slabs of wood up to twelve feet long lashed to ordinary winter boots. Propulsion was achieved by using a single, stout pole that the skier pushed into the snow, alternating sides, to move forward—kind of like poling a flatboat

Soldiers pose on a porch at Fort Yellowstone in Mammoth with bison heads confiscated from infamous poacher Ed Howell.
PHOTOGRAPHER UNKNOWN, 1894. NPS.GOV.

through the swamp. Hough spent a few days getting used to the skis, which made for a pretty funny segment of his series. Sometimes a fall would entail up to an hour of struggling and squirming to get his feet under him so he could stand. Without the skis, he reported, travel was impossible: "In the summer one rides through the Park in comparative ease. In the winter one cannot even walk."

The park was devoid of visitors in winter, and Mammoth Springs Hotel was empty except for the winter keeper and his wife, so Hough bunked at Captain Anderson's quarters for a few days. The writer's assignment included photographing as much game as he could, and his initial foray into the park brought him within range of four hundred head of antelope, which, he wrote, was probably the entire population within the park. He also reported sightings of bighorn sheep and bald eagles on his trip in from Cinnabar.

It was during these initial few days in Yellowstone that Hough met F. Jay Haynes, the famed photographer whose photos of the park and its wildlife had already become legend. Haynes joined Hough and Hofer on their expedition, capturing many indelible images of their adventure. Other men had ventured into the park in winter to create maps and document the otherworldly thermal features, but this was one of the first, and most important, expeditions mounted specifically to count and photograph the large animals that inhabited the park. Bison, elk, and other wild game tended to cluster together at lower elevations in winter, which made the counting easier. It also made it easier to apprehend the man responsible for slaughtering hundreds of bison without giving a second thought to the survival of the herd.

Captain Anderson was well acquainted with the exploits of Ed Howell and knew that the man went in and out of the northeast sector of the park from Cooke City, the mining town where he was based. Anderson sent scout Felix Burgess out to the Pelican Valley to search for Howell's camp. Just days earlier, Burgess had accompanied Billy Hofer to investigate the carcasses of four dead bison found near pits dug in the snow. The heads and hides were intact, suggesting that a poacher had been spooked and abandoned his bounty in mid-poach. Either that, Captain Anderson later surmised, or the buffalo had been shot just for kicks. Burgess dutifully returned to the valley and found the tracks of the poacher. Ski tracks in the snow lasted for weeks, as the skis compressed the snow under the weight of the skier, and when the surrounding snow began to melt off or blow away, the ridges of compressed snow would remain, making for an easy trail to follow.

Burgess discovered Howell's tepee and a cache of buffalo heads that had been wrapped in gunny sacks and hoisted into the trees, out of reach of the wolves. He was searching the camp, which was surely Howell's, when he heard six rifle shots nearby. Moving through the timber toward the direction of the shots, he saw Howell some four hundred yards away. He also counted five buffalo that had been felled by the six shots. Armed with only a six-shot revolver, Burgess would have to exit the forest and cross a good amount of open ground to arrest the man. A stiff wind was blowing in his face, and Howell was already bent over his work, skinning the first bison. Howell's dog lay curled up next to a bison carcass, unaware of Burgess's scent, being upwind of the scout. Howell's rifle was leaning against a dead bison fifteen feet away. Moving as fast as he could on his skis, Burgess somehow jumped a ten-foot-wide ditch and got the drop on Howell. With the howling wind covering the sound of Burgess's approach, the poacher's dog never barked. Burgess drew his revolver and called out to Howell to raise his hands. Howell stood and looked at Burgess stupidly, probably astonished to see another person in this part of the park. Burgess commanded him to drop his knife. "I see I was subject to the drop," Howell later told Hough, "so I let go my knife and came along."

Burgess summoned his companion, Private Troike, who had stayed in the trees. They marched Howell without much trouble back to the Lake Hotel near the north end of Yellowstone Lake, where they phoned Captain Anderson with the news: they had captured Yellowstone's most infamous poacher.

Anderson ordered that the prisoner be brought to the army post at Mammoth, which they did by way of the Canyon Hotel and Norris. Howell was reportedly gregarious and upbeat, no doubt untroubled by the threat of punishment. He knew there would be little or none. Under military regulations the prisoner could be mistreated a bit while in custody, but then he would be escorted out of the park. Anderson—and, notably, Hough—knew full well that Howell would return to the park sooner or later and continue his wanton slaughter of the increasingly rare bison, as there was little deterrent against it.

Hough later reported that Anderson, thoroughly disgusted with Howell and hamstrung by the lack of grounds on which to punish him, ordered a party to return to Howell's camp to burn what remained to the ground. The cadre was unable to find the site, even though Private Troike, who had been there, was part of the team. Howell's gear had already been confiscated, which didn't seem to ruffle the prisoner too much. His possessions were worth $26.50, and he stood to make up to $2,000 for the bison he'd planned to bring in, he told his captors. He bragged that he might return to Yellowstone; he hadn't made up his mind. Anderson and his men found Howell's gloating nearly unbearable but couldn't do much about it.

Hough had just reached Norris when Howell and his captors arrived at that encampment, and within a few hours he'd written up a story and filed it via telephone with *Forest and Stream*. The story gained traction and was quickly picked up by other publications, and the tale of the relentless poacher and his decimation of the remaining bison population was national news. But what could be done? Hough had learned firsthand that it was impossible for Captain Anderson and two troops of soldiers to stop the poaching. Although the act that established the national park in 1872 included a section that prohibited hunting "for the purpose of merchandising or profit," the illegal trade of bison heads and hides went on unchecked. Conservationists, once made aware that the country was in the process of killing off an entire species, had already made some efforts to slow, if not reverse, what seemed to be the inevitable extinction of the American bison. There were a few small herds here and there, in places like North Dakota and Texas, but it seemed as if the wild buffalo's days were numbered.

When word got out about Howell's capture and the lack of any law in place that had enough teeth to provide a deterrent, George Bird Grinnell went into action. He was an avid hunter and, like most serious sportsmen, a conservationist. With Theodore Roosevelt, Grinnell had established the Boone and Crockett Club. When Hough's report from Yellowstone brought the buffalo's plight into focus, Grinnell went immediately to Washington, DC, and began to twist arms. Within a month, the Lacey Act was enacted by Congress, providing protections for all wildlife, fish, and plants within the national park. Anyone caught hunting bison would now face stiff fines and possibly years in prison.

The last remaining herd of wild bison in America had dwindled, by Hough's thoroughly researched count, to 150 animals. In 1895 the Smithsonian Institution suggested an enclosure that could protect the native bison within the park. Congress allotted the funds and a pasture was fenced off on Alum Creek. Attempts were made to bait the animals into the enclosure, but the efforts eventually failed and the project was abandoned. For a few years bison were herded up to higher elevations in the summer to relieve pressure on the plant life being grazed in the pastures of the Lamar Valley and Hayden Valley. With poaching eventually diminishing by the early 1900s, and with the addition of a few animals from the Goodnight Herd in Texas, the population leveled off and slowly began to rebound. Thanks to the efforts of C. J. "Buffalo" Jones, a trapper from Colorado, the Lamar Valley herd had grown to 259 bison by 1915. The bison were fed hay in the winter to keep them from leaving the park in search of food. Bison wranglers kept predators at bay, and the Lamar and Pelican Valley herds were eventually merged. By 1930 there were 1,100 bison in Yellowstone Park.

Today the Yellowstone bison comprise two distinct herds: the Hayden Valley herd and the Pelican/Lamar Valley herd. The population is robust enough that controversial practices like buffalo hunts and hazing by Montana's FWP out of concern for brucellosis are not seen as an immediate threat to the species. Yellowstone's bison might cause trouble when they wander out of the park, but today they remain one of the most reliable sights in Yellowstone, a breathtaking symbol not just of a Wild West lost to the haze of history but also of a culture that has the ability to see the error of its ways, even before it's almost too late, and take action to preserve one of its most cherished national treasures.

CHAPTER 10

Captured by Indians

A visit to Yellowstone typically includes a raft of warnings about the natural hazards that abound in the park and how to avoid them. Hikers carry bear spray, and some announce their presence to any unseen bruins by shaking bear bells or singing in a robust voice. Visitors should keep at least one hundred yards between themselves and a bear. It's recommended that bison also be given a wide berth—twenty-five yards at least. While bison are accustomed to having people around, their "gentle giant" appearance is deceptive. They're cantankerous, quick, and powerful. A bison can run forty-five miles per hour, and visitors have actually perished at the business end of a bison's horns because they invaded the animal's personal space. Moose and elk will also charge, especially if you put yourself between a female and her offspring. And it's not just the megafauna that can ruin your vacation. Sudden storms have caught many boaters by surprise on Yellowstone Lake, and many tourists have wandered off the boardwalks or trails in the geyser areas and paid the price by being seriously injured or even killed when stepping or falling into a scalding hot pool.

But it's a pretty good bet that no one warns you to keep an eye out for marauding Indians in the park. For one unfortunate woman, however, a Yellowstone vacation for her and her husband became a nightmare of horrific violence and terror when their party found themselves in the wrong place at the wrong time and were savagely attacked by a band of Indians. What was to have been an idyllic trip to celebrate the couple's second anniversary became a grim ordeal when she was captured and held hostage while her husband was shot and left for dead.

The year was 1877, and Emma Carpenter Cowan was eager to get back to Yellowstone. As a young girl growing up in Virginia City, she'd heard tales from an old trapper who held her and her siblings spellbound with fantastic stories of "fountains of boiling water . . . thrown hundreds of feet in the air, pools of water within whose limpid depths tints of the various rainbows were reflected." Her father dismissed the stories as fanciful tales spun in the cracked mind of a doddering old man, but young Emma latched onto the images of an incredible world of natural wonder. In 1873, after her family had moved to Helena, she finally got her chance to visit the area known as Wonderland. Yellowstone had been established as the first national park the year before, but only a few hundred visitors had been to the park at that point. Emma traveled into the park through Gardiner and spent two weeks marveling at the colorful, steaming features at Mammoth Hot Springs. She made a few friends at the hotel and spent her days dipping handkerchiefs and other items into the mineral waters of the travertine terraces. They would become encrusted, creating a unique souvenir for Emma to take home.

As much as she enjoyed the scenery and the inimitable mineral formations of the hot springs, Emma longed to take the hundred-mile round-trip horseback journey to the Upper Geyser Basin, where the brilliantly colored hot pools and impressive exploding fountains were found. She heard dozens of stories from visitors who'd returned from the area and struggled to describe the incredible wonders they'd seen. One phrase kept cropping up in their accounts: "You must see them for yourself!" Emma vowed that one day she would. Four years later she would get her chance.

While Emma Cowan and her husband, George, were preparing to leave their home in Radersburg, Montana, for her long-awaited return to Yellowstone, the Nez Perce War was heating up in the southwest part of the state, about two hundred miles west of the park. A band of Nez Perce Indians, led by Chief Joseph, was working its way eastward from the Bitterroot Valley toward the Big Hole Valley, with the US Army hot on their trail. The Nez Perce were non-treaty Indians, having rejected attempts by the US government to remove them from their ancestral lands, in itself a violation of the Treaty of Walla Walla, an agreement forged in 1855 that would have ceded 7.5 million acres of land to the government with the understanding that the natives would retain the rights to hunt and fish on the land. Looking to head east and gain support from the Crow tribe, the Nez Perce moved their band (which numbered about 750 men, women, and children) north through Idaho and into Montana through Lolo Pass. They'd been fighting occasional skirmishes with a regiment of soldiers and, after a brief battle at Fort Fizzle in late July, turned south to head down the Bitterroot Valley. Around this time Looking Glass assumed leadership from Chief Joseph, and he'd sent word ahead to the settlers of the valley that his people were not interested in engaging the locals in any warfare. The Nez Perce were able to travel through the area without incident, even stopping briefly to trade with a few merchants and trappers. They crossed a mountain range, probably through Skalkaho Pass, and headed for the Big Hole Valley. At this point Looking Glass was convinced that General Oliver Otis Howard and his men were far behind, so the band relaxed their defensive measures a bit. Once they reached the Big Hole, they set up their eighty-nine tepees in an open meadow near the Big Hole River, just across the water from a forested hillside. Worn out by the relentless pursuit of the army, the tribal members rested their weary bones and replenished their supply of tepee poles from lodgepole pines in the surrounding forest.

That night, as they slept, they had no idea that Colonel John Gibbon, who had followed their trail from Fort Shaw and picked up the scent in the Bitterroot, had discovered the camp. He was marshaling his troops on the hillside across the river from the temporary village. He'd brought more than two hundred men with him, along with a howitzer that shot twelve-pound iron balls.

Just before dawn some soldiers approached the camp on foot and encountered an elderly Nez Perce man down by the river. They killed him and forded the waist-deep water, pouring into the camp, firing at anything that moved—women, children, warriors—and reportedly aimed low, being sure to hit those lying down in their tepees. The Nez Perce rose to fight, and one of Gibbon's lieutenants, James Bradley, was killed by a Nez Perce bullet. With their leader dead, Bradley's squad abandoned the attack, falling back and leaving the northern part of the camp open, which the Nez Perce quickly used for refuge and regrouping. Gibbon himself was hit in the leg. Twenty minutes after his troops entered the village, he ordered a retreat back across the river to a wooded area about four hundred yards away. There his men dug rifle pits and settled into a sniping exchange throughout the morning while they waited for the howitzer crew to move the cannon into position.

The Nez Perce, with cover fire from their snipers, were able to pack up, gather their herd of horses, and flee to the south. They traveled eighteen miles to Lake Creek, where they set up camp, this time diligently using all their defensive tactics such as scouts and sentries. Now they were better outfitted for protection, having collected several firearms that were dropped by soldiers in the fighting. It is estimated that they suffered between seventy and ninety casualties at the Big Hole battlefield. The wives of Chief Joseph and his brother Ollokot were wounded but survived the battle. Gibbon's faction lost twenty-nine men, including six civilian volunteers. Most of the howitzer crew were killed or wounded after getting off only two or three shots, none of which did any damage.

Nez Perce warriors remained engaged with the army snipers, while Gibbon, fearing that he was outnumbered, hunkered down and waited for reinforcements to arrive. His men had little food or water and spent a pretty tough night on the mountain. Howard and his regiment would catch up to them the following morning.

Having suffered such great losses in the surprise attack, the Nez Perce would no longer trust any white man, no matter what promises were made. Their only chance to escape the fate of the reservation was to make it to Canada. The warriors left the battle sometime in the night to rejoin their tribe as they headed east toward Yellowstone.

Around this time, Emma Carpenter Cowan, her husband George, brother Frank, sister Ida, and five others were on their way to Yellowstone. As the only woman among the travelers, Emma had convinced her parents to allow thirteen-year-old Ida to come along so that Emma could have some female companionship. After the original number of participants ballooned to nine people, they secured a wagon team and a cook to accompany them. They spent their first night camped in Three Forks and then followed the Madison River south. They got as far as a small mining town south of Norris, Montana, where Emma and most of the party arrived well before the supply wagon. They had a meal at the local hotel, where the locals, upon learning of their destination, warned them of the bands of dangerous Indians roaming through the park. The next day they passed through Ennis and came to Henrys Lake, where the fishing was tremendous. Dismissing the Indian stories as an empty local scare, they spent several sunny days enjoying the lake. A few of the men had brought fiddles and a guitar, and sing-alongs around the campfire were a nightly pleasure.

They departed Henrys Lake on August 13 to tackle the seven-thousand-foot Targhee Pass, coming out at West Yellowstone, where they entered the park. Once again moving along the Madison River, they reached the Firehole River, where they turned south and at last reached their destination: the Lower Geyser Basin. After a four-year wait and a nine-day journey, Emma had finally returned to Yellowstone.

As many visitors do even today, the party established a base camp that would act as a hub for their excursions to different areas of the park. Fountain Geyser was as far as a wagon could go into the park, so from there they would continue on horseback. While camp was being set up and supplies for a short excursion were being loaded onto pack horses, a small party from Bear Gulch rode in, led by seasoned guide George Huston. When the Radersburg party learned that they were also headed to the Upper Geyser Basin, they decided to travel together. This is when Emma and her group first learned of the furious battle that had been fought between the US Army and the Nez Perce at the Big Hole Valley. Huston assured the group that they were in no danger from the Indians, as the savages would never enter the park because their "superstitious minds associate it with hell, by reason of its geysers and hot springs." Still game but a little nervous, the party rode to the Upper Geyser Basin. Frank and a few others split off to travel to Yellowstone Lake and the Falls, guided by Huston, agreeing to rendezvous back at their base camp near Fountain Geyser.

Back at camp on Thursday, August 23, the Radersburg travelers, having enjoyed a satisfying sojourn in Yellowstone, made plans to leave for home the following day, which was the second anniversary of Emma and George Cowan's wedding. A celebration was planned. Emma awoke in the morning to the sound of voices, but not that of her husband whispering "happy anniversary" in her ear. She peeked out of the tent and saw a couple of Indians who had entered the camp and were speaking in their guttural native tongue. She awoke George, who crawled out of the tent to talk with the interlopers. He was relieved to find they were Nez Perce, who had always been peaceful in their dealings with white settlers.

It probably escaped George that these particular natives had been forced off their ancestral land, harassed, hunted, and shot at by the US Cavalry during the ongoing Indian Wars. The warriors, especially, had become hostile toward white men. One of the Nez Perce in the Radersburg camp that morning was Yellow Wolf, who was leading a small scout team into the park to find a safe passage that would take them farther east, where they could seek refuge with the Crow Indians in eastern Montana. Fortunately for Emma and her group, Yellow Wolf was one member of the tribe who saw the cavalry, not the white civilians, as their enemy.

George and the other men thought the best plan would be to break camp immediately and head north, as the Indians were coming in from the west. By this time another couple dozen Indians had arrived in the camp, with more coming behind them. As the campers packed up, A. J. Arnold began passing out sugar and flour to assuage the Indians. When George discovered his friend's largesse, he lost his cool and ordered the Indians to leave their camp. In the tense situation, this was not the smartest move. As Emma would later write, "[T]his materially lessened his chances of escape."

Packed up and ready to ride, the Radersburg party trekked north, followed by forty or fifty Indians. Emma assumed that they were just going the same way until a few miles up the trail, when suddenly a group of sixty warriors materialized out of the surrounding forest upon a command given by one of the Indians traveling with them. Another of the mounted Indians pointed to the native who had given the command and said in English, "Him, Joseph." The Radersburg party was astonished to realize that they had been traveling in the company of the famed Nez

Perce leader, Chief Joseph himself. Their party was ordered to turn around and follow the trail toward Mary Lake. After a few miles the wagons were abandoned, and Emma and her crew could take only the supplies and possessions they could carry on horseback over the timber-strewn trail. During a stop for lunch, an Indian named Poker Joe, who spoke English, made an offer to the Radersburg party: if they would trade their horses for the Indians' worn-out nags, they would be free to go. The travelers had no choice but to comply. While the exchange was under way, William Dingee and A. J. Arnold slipped away into the forest and headed west. The rest of the Radersburg travelers, unaware of their comrades' escape, mounted the haggard tribal steeds and began riding south toward the Lower Geyser Basin. After riding for a couple of miles, the group began to allow themselves some hope that they'd make it home alive.

Their hopes faded when they discovered a band of warriors on their tail. They were stopped and told that the chief wanted to speak with them again. Hearts sinking, Emma and her family and friends turned around and headed back up the trail. Were they being toyed with? The idea that they'd escape this predicament alive began to fade.

Gunshots rang out. Two Indians were barreling down the trail toward them. George took a bullet in the thigh and fell out of his saddle. He hit the ground, collapsed, and tumbled down a hill, where he came to rest against a pine tree. More shots were fired as Emma leaped from her horse and ran to her husband, only to see blood spurting from the wound in his leg. Ida worked her way down to join her sister, and Emma told her sister and wounded husband to keep quiet and just wait out the melee. When the women turned from George to look uphill, "Every gun of the whole party of Indians was leveled on us three," as Emma later wrote. "The holes in those gun barrels looked as big as saucers."

As one Indian tried to drag Emma away from George, Emma saw another level a large navy pistol at her husband's head. A shot exploded, George's head rocked back, and a stream of blood oozed from under his hat. Ida screamed as other Indians began heaving rocks at George's head. On the day when Emma should have been celebrating two years of marriage to her beloved, she instead was witnessing (as she supposed) his murder at the hands of the Yellowstone savages.

She passed out.

During the attack, Charles Mann and Henry Myers managed to escape. Albert Oldham had been shot in the face and lay slumped against a tree. When Emma regained consciousness, her brother Frank appeared at her side and told her the Indians had said the party would suffer no further violence. They were still held captive, though, and were ordered to move along the trail toward the Nez Perce village in the Hayden Valley. George and Albert were left for dead.

As they traveled north and east through Yellowstone Park, they joined up with many other groups of Indians. Eventually the exodus had swelled to nearly six hundred Indians as the Nez Perce moved along a narrow trail through the forest that normally carried just a few tourists. When their captors discovered that Frank knew the area trails, he was forced to walk point, leading the entire procession. Emma had also gotten separated from Ida. At the end of a long day of hiking, they reached the Hayden Valley. Emma was reunited with Frank and assured by Chief Joseph that she would be able to see her young sister in the morning. Numb with grief over losing George, she sat up all night by the glowing embers of the fire with Frank, wondering what their fate would be in the coming days.

In the morning she was indeed reunited with Ida, who was ecstatic to see that her sister was still alive. Poker Joe mobilized the assorted bands of Nez Perce, and the group moved north through the Hayden Valley. They crossed the Yellowstone River near Mud Geyser, and then they stopped to set up camp for dinner. The Indians also held a council, where the fate of the white captives would be decided. Emma, Ida, and Frank were the only remaining members of the Radersburg party. The tribal council passed around a pipe, and if Chief Joseph smoked, it meant that the white settlers could go free. He smoked. Frank, however, was commanded to stay with the tribe to serve as scout, along with John Shively, another white man who had been captured. Shaky from lack of food and grief-stricken over her murdered husband, Emma nonetheless put her foot down, refusing to leave without her brother. The Indians talked it over and agreed to let Frank go, too.

With two beat horses and a modicum of supplies, the surviving Radersburg travelers were guided by Poker Joe to the Yellowstone River. Their Indian ally bade them farewell and told them to stick to the trail along the river, which would take them to Bozeman in three days if they didn't stop. With Frank on foot and Ida and Emma riding on their worn-out horses, however, they made slow progress.

The next day, August 26, they made it to Tower Falls, where they encountered Lieutenant Charles B. Schofield and his soldiers, who'd been tracking the Nez Perce out of Fort Ellis. Frank informed Schofield of their plight and said that they were the only survivors of their original party. A short time later a man ran into the soldiers' camp and announced that his own camping party out of Helena had been attacked near the falls, and he was the lone survivor. The Carpenter trio was eager to move on. After a dinner at the camp, they were supplied with fresh horses and provisions and, along with the surviving Helena man (named Pfister), set out for Mammoth Hot Springs.

Upon reaching Mammoth, Frank telegraphed their brother George in Helena and told of the horrors of the attack in Yellowstone. George Cowan and Albert Oldham had been killed, he said.

Two days later they reached Bozeman. From there Emma and Ida set out for her parents' ranch near Townsend, while Frank prepared to return to Yellowstone to recover the bodies of his friend and brother-in-law.

Three days earlier, unbeknownst to the surviving Radersburg party, Charles Mann and Henry Myers were found by General Howard's scouts near Madison Junction. At Henrys Lake, Howard's soldiers also came upon William Dingee and A. J. Arnold, the pair who'd slipped away during the initial skirmish with the Indian scouts in the Radersburg camp. They'd traveled forty miles in four days on foot, including hiking over Targhee Pass. As General Howard and his troops continued to move through the park in pursuit of the Nez Perce, they also scooped up Albert Oldham, who had not only survived being shot in the face but also managed to travel twenty miles to the Madison road.

The most amazing tale of survival, however, belonged to George Cowan. He somehow survived the point-blank pistol shot to the head and avoided bleeding out from his thigh wound. As he summoned his strength and began crawling up the embankment to the trail, a lone passing warrior spotted him and plugged him in the left hip. Left for dead once again, George regained consciousness and dragged himself ten miles back to their original campsite at the Lower Geyser Basin. It took him four days. After a day of rest and some coffee made from a few beans he'd found, he managed to crawl several more miles to the bank of the Firehole River, where his body finally gave out. He collapsed under a tree near the road. Later that day he was discovered by a pair of General Howard's men, who were dumbfounded by George's story of survival. The men had been sent to find George's body and bury him. George asked about the fate of his wife, but the men had no information. The scouts had little to offer him at all, except for a blanket and some food. They had to move on, but they assured George that the full command was only a day behind them. They built a small fire for the wounded man and left.

Under these circumstances, you would think that rescue would be imminent, that George would soon receive medical attention and be reunited with his lovely Emma. You would be wrong. George was having the bad day of all bad days. When he awoke from his slumber, he was surrounded by flames. The scouts had unknowingly laid him on a bed of dry vegetable mold, which was extremely dry in the late-summer heat and had been ignited by the campfire. George managed to extricate himself from the blaze, but not before suffering severe burns. The following day General Howard's command did indeed arrive. George's wounds were dressed, and he was transported to Mammoth Hot Springs. From there he would be sent to Bozeman and then home to Radersburg and Emma. His bereaved wife, needless to say, was overjoyed to hear the news of George's remarkable survival.

But it would be another couple of weeks before the pair would be reunited. George was to have reached Bozeman by September 19, but his frail health had required a stay at Bottler's Ranch in the Paradise Valley until he could recuperate sufficiently to travel. Unable to wait, Emma procured a double carriage and drove down to the Paradise Valley. By the time she found him he seemed to be able to travel, so they loaded him up in a bed in the back of the carriage and headed for home. She was accompanied by a driver and A. J. Arnold. They would head out to Bozeman and then turn north toward Helena.

Just seven miles from Bozeman, they were rolling along a rocky canyon road that traversed a steep slope when a pole strap snapped, spooking the horses. They broke the carriage tongue and bolted, throwing all of the carriage's occupants out onto the hillside. The carriage tumbled down the ravine and crashed at the bottom of the canyon. Everyone survived, but many of George's wounds had reopened. The driver borrowed a passing rider's horse and raced to nearby Fort Ellis, where he sent an ambulance to fetch George.

When George was unloaded from the ambulance and deposited in a hotel bed in Bozeman, Emma figured that they were home free. Once her hapless husband was stabilized, they could continue on their way home, just a couple days' ride. Arnold came into the room to dress George's wounds for his emaciated, frail friend. Unfortunately, as Arnold sat on the edge of the bed, the frame collapsed, throwing poor George onto the floor. Emma later wrote, "This sudden and unexpected fall, in his enfeebled state, nearly finished him."

George would need another week of recovery before he was strong enough to travel home to Radersburg. The string of incredible bad luck and George's ability to cheat death several times over was mind-blowing to Emma and the others. "Had I been morbidly inclined," she wrote, "I might have conceived the idea that some avenging Nemesis was following in his foot-steps, which nothing but the forfeit of his life would satisfy." Amazingly, George eventually made a full recovery.

Emma Carpenter Cowan and her husband George return to visit the spot in Yellowstone where they were captured by Nez Perce Indians.
PHOTOGRAPHER UNKNOWN, 1905. GALLATIN HISTORICAL SOCIETY AND MUSEUM.

Hiram Chittenden, Yellowstone Park historian, invited George and Emma Cowan to return to Yellowstone in 1901 to revisit the sites where their hair-raising adventure had taken place in August 1877. The episode was deeply embedded in the couple's memories, and Chittenden wrote of George in particular, "His recollections of localities was astonishingly vivid and accurate." Their captivity and George's unlikely tale of survival was a sensation, receiving coverage in the national press upon their return to Radersburg. The Cowans, who now had three children, moved to Spokane in 1910, and Emma became something of a celebrity as her legend grew. Somewhere along the line the press turned their two-year anniversary into their honeymoon, which probably made for more sensational headlines: "Honeymooners Captured by Indians in Yellowstone!" Although the details would become scrambled as the story matured into legend, Emma Carpenter Cowan had survived an ordeal that few of us could even imagine.

CHAPTER 11

Nature's Laundromat

Jim Bridger famously called Yellowstone "the place where Hell bubbled up." It's a pretty spot-on description for the eye-popping geothermal features scattered across this mountain plateau. Half the world's geysers are found here, and a day spent wandering around the caldera section of the park makes it easy to understand why early reports of these fantastic steam fountains were dismissed as fanciful tales cooked up by the mind of a mountain man too long in the wild with nothing but a sack of dried buffalo meat and his fertile imagination. Now, of course, millions of people from around the globe can attest to their magnificence, having witnessed the grandeur of Old Faithful or the rumbling menace of Steamboat Geyser, which last blew its top in 2018. The steaming fumaroles, the bubbling mud pots, the Technicolor hot pools—they all represent nature at its most flamboyant as the earth literally blows off some steam.

But visitors to the world's oldest national park—there were 4.1 million in 2017—haven't always treated these spectacular geologic oddities with the respect and reverence we show them today. It seems every year that there's a handful of knuckleheads who disregard their own safety and risk their lives to get closer to the hot springs or geysers than is prudent (or allowed). When a tourist from the Netherlands crashed a drone into Grand Prismatic Spring in the summer of 2015, he probably wasn't thinking that his actions could cause irreparable damage to one of the most beautiful natural sights on the planet. The following year, at the same spot, four men shot a video of themselves leaving the boardwalk to tromp across the fragile surface surrounding the hot spring. Sure, they risked their lives, but they also may have damaged the microbial mats that make the world's third-largest hot spring such a spectacular sight and popular tourist attraction. Park rangers are vigilant, signs are all over the place warning visitors to stay on the boardwalks, and fines for those who disregard the rules are stiff. Unfortunately, the boneheaded side of human nature can't be entirely contained. You can't fix stupid.

Less than a hundred years ago this kind of behavior would have been considered no big deal. People routinely went too close to geysers and hot springs, causing themselves grievous injury and even death. Common sense? Not that common. Knowing now how delicate the ecosystem is that keeps the hot springs and geysers in their natural state, it's fairly shocking to hear about some of the stunts that Yellowstone tourists used to pull before rules and regulations were put in place to help protect visitors and thermal features alike. For one, people put all manner of things into Yellowstone's geysers, from fish to soap and clothes to couches. Would you believe that Old Faithful, the grand old dame of Upper Geyser Basin, was actually used as a laundry? That's been the legend for almost a century and a half. Is it true? Well, that all depends on who is telling the tale.

Stories abound of Yellowstone's geysers and hot springs being used to launder clothing. In Black Sand Basin you'll find a small hot spring called Handkerchief Pool. In the early twentieth century it was one of the most popular attractions in the park, even rivaling Old Faithful in the number of visitors it would attract. People would walk right up to the edge of the ten-foot-wide hot pool, which had been ringed in concrete, and drop their soiled hankies into the steaming water. The handkerchief would be sucked down into the depths and emerge in an eruption a few minutes later, boiled clean. Park rangers took to demonstrating the pool's cleaning power. Soon people began to throw all manner of things into the water. Coins, bottles, pins, rocks, even a horseshoe were tossed into the small spring. By 1928 the damage was done. Handkerchief Pool went dormant, its thermal workings destroyed by all the foreign elements introduced into its fragile system.

In the Upper Geyser Basin Loop (home to Old Faithful), there is a small hot spring called Chinese Spring. It is the site where, according to the *Yellowstone Naturalist*, an Asian immigrant actually ran a laundry service, using the superheated water to clean clothing. However, sometimes a spring turns out to be a geyser, which he found out the hard way when the spring suddenly erupted, sending his washing flying through the air. His repeated introduction of clothing into the geyser probably damaged the interior structure, as the eruptions slowed down to the point that it's now considered a hot spring. There is no recorded or photographic evidence of this laundry, but it lends itself to the persistent legend of the geyser laundry phenomenon.

Today throwing clothes into one of Yellowstone's geysers seems unthinkable. In the early days of the park, though, people didn't know any better. There's something about human nature that spurs some people to commit vandalism and destruction when a natural wonder is discovered, especially in the European Americans who came west to capitalize on the wide-open spaces they thought were theirs for the taking. Rather than bringing a reverence for the land, as was embraced by the inhabitants who'd already been here for several millennia, their impulse was to dominate and destroy. There's a great example of this impulse in Stone Mountain, Georgia, where a quartz monzonite dome rises nearly nine hundred feet above the surrounding area about ten miles from Atlanta. Part of the Blue Ridge Mountains, it was formed more than three hundred million years ago. Native Americans in the area had used the granite monolith for a meeting and ceremonial place for generations. Shortly after a pair of Atlanta businessmen gained control of the mountain and its surrounding land, they hired stone workers to carve a 150-foot-tall depiction of Confederate generals into the side of it. Now you can grab a hot dog and settle in on the lawn of Stone Mountain Park when the sun goes down and watch a laser light show projected on the side of the mountain, complete with a pop country music soundtrack and commercials for Coca-Cola.

Were it not for emerging science and a better understanding of the geology of Yellowstone's massive dormant volcano, who knows what kind of crass commercialism may have been inflicted on the park? Thankfully, the National Park Service led the way in protecting Yellowstone's fragile ecosystem, but not before damage was done to a number of its geothermal features, like Handkerchief Pool. In the park's first fifty years or so, geysers were susceptible to the "experiments" of visitors who wanted to see what would happen when they threw various objects into them. Minute Geyser was named for its habit of erupting every sixty seconds, blowing a plume some fifty feet into the air. People began throwing rocks into the vent, and before long the geyser was clogged with debris; now only a smaller vent erupts—and sporadically at that.

Morning Glory is probably the most famous of all the features that have been forever altered by the thoughtless act of throwing foreign objects into it. The gorgeous, cerulean pool in the Upper Geyser Basin was named by Mrs. E. N. McGowan, wife of assistant superintendent Charles McGowan, in 1883. She called it "Convolutus," the Latin name for the flower she thought it resembled. It occasionally erupts as a geyser, usually when there's earthquake activity. The beautiful blue color comes from the thermophilic bacteria that thrive at this pool's particular temperature, but the tint has faded over time, and the surrounding crust has turned yellow and orange. Scientists have determined that the color change is a direct result of tourists throwing things into the spring. As the debris settles into the bottom of the pool, it clogs the vents that feed superheated water from below. Photosynthetic microorganisms began to thrive in the pool, changing the color of the water from a tropical blue to a gnarly green. All kinds of items have been tossed into the embattled pool, including, reportedly, a couch.

In 1950 park workers siphoned water from the spring in an attempt to clear out some of the junk. Morning Glory erupted, shooting out handkerchiefs, socks, bath towels, and $94.37 in coins. In all,

112 different objects as well as the coins were removed from the hot spring. The pool is widely known today as "Faded Glory."

To understand how introducing foreign objects into a spring or geyser causes damage to the system, it helps to know exactly how Yellowstone's thermal features work. Yellowstone sits atop an active volcano, and hot magma deep under the earth's surface keeps the underground water superheated. A "plumbing system" of sinter-lined chambers and shafts collects draining surface water from streams and rivers and water draining back from previous eruptions. The cooler water mixes with hot water from below, filling the chambers. The farther underground the heated water is, the more pressure is exerted, keeping it from boiling even as it surpasses two hundred degrees Fahrenheit. This superheated water combines with the collected surface water in the sealed system and builds pressure until it is released upward in a jet of steam and water. Geysers differ from hot springs at this point because the water is squeezed through a constricted space near the surface, increasing the pressure much like when you hold your thumb over the end of a garden hose to create a spray. Water shoots out of the geyser faster than it can be refilled from below, and as heat and pressure decrease, the fountain eventually subsides and the whole cycle starts again. It can happen within a few minutes, or, as with Steamboat Geyser, several years may go by between eruptions.

The plumbing systems of geysers are complex and sensitive, and the smallest obstruction can affect the flow of water and steam, resulting in fewer eruptions or even the inability of the geyser to function at all. It's unlikely that the members of Frank Carpenter's party were aware of any of this when they visited Yellowstone in 1877, five years after it was established as a national park. He'd traveled from Raders-burg, Montana, with his two sisters and a few friends, and when they reached the Upper Geyser Basin they became infatuated with the geysers and hot springs. Once they got to Old Faithful, they decided to experiment with the geyser. Having not had a chance to launder their clothing during the trip, it was suggested by a guide named George Huston that they throw their grungy things into the geyser's maw. They bundled up their jackets, blouses, and handkerchiefs, tied them off in a pillowcase, and heaved them into the geyser's opening. The water level continued to drop, sucking their clothing into the earth. When the geyser went off, Carpenter later wrote, "the clothes, mixed in every conceivable shape, shoot up to a distance of a hundred feet and fall with a splash in the basins below. The water subsides, and we fish out the clothing, which, we find as nice and clean as a Chinaman could wash it with a week's scrubbing."

Carpenter's use of a nineteenth-century stereotype aside, it's an astonishing account of a blatant abuse of a rare natural feature. And stuffing clothing down into Old Faithful wasn't enough for this group. "We fill[ed] it to the top with at least a thousand pounds of stones, trees and stumps," he wrote. The geyser erupted an hour later, sending debris eighty feet into the air.

Henry Bird Calfee, a Yellowstone photographer in the late 1870s, was another park visitor who chronicled using Old Faithful as a laundromat:

I . . . went up to the Old Faithful Geyser to whom we had delivered our washing the morning before starting out. I

A park ranger demonstrates the cleaning power of Handkerchief Pool in Black Sand Basin.

HAYNES STUDIO, PHOTOGRAPHER UNKNOWN, DATE UNKNOWN. HAYNES FOUNDATION COLLECTION, MONTANA HISTORICAL SOCIETY RESEARCH CENTER PHOTOGRAPH ARCHIVES, HELENA, MONTANA.

found it all nicely washed and lying on his pearly pavement ready for delivery. Our linen and cotton garments, which had been stiff and black with dirt lay there as white as the driven snow and our woolen clothes were as clean as could be. But o my, imagine them in that mammoth unpatented washing machine boiling for one solid hour and then imagine my one hundred and sixty-five-pound carcass inside of a suit of underwear scarcely large enough for a ten-year-old boy. I said to Old Faithful, you are a mighty good laundryman but you will not do up my flannels anymore. I went back to camp regretting that we couldn't stay in his vicinity long enough to patronize him again.

Soldiers of the US Army, who served to oversee the park until the formation of the National Park Service in 1916, were frequent users of Old Faithful's churning, superheated water. It was *de rigueur* for soldiers to routinely stuff their uniforms and other clothing into the geyser and wait for it to be agitated and then expelled in a mighty blast. They would then gather the steam-cleaned items and lay them out to dry. Reportedly, cotton and linen garments were cleaned and unharmed, but for some reason anything made of wool was shredded to bits. Those in the know with textiles can tell you that cotton can withstand much higher temperatures than other fabrics.

There are also several instances on record of laundry soap being poured into geysers, but it had nothing to do with removing stains or making whites their whitest. Park guides in the early 1900s would sometimes pour some laundry soap into the opening of a

geyser to jump-start an eruption for the gathered crowd. The sur-
factant effect of the soap reduced the surface tension between water
molecules deep in the geyser's plumbing, allowing the boiling water
to convert into steam. Showtime! It's doubtful that the people who
did this understood the science; they just knew that it made the
thing blow. The practice picked up steam, so to speak, with visitors.
For a while the general stores in the park had a hard time keeping
laundry detergent on the shelves. Today such a violation of the natural balance of a geyser would be unthinkable.

Early visitors found other ways to take advantage of the scalding
water spurting from the earth in Yellowstone. Going all the way
back to the Washburn-Langford-Doane Expedition of 1870, explorers and mountain men have claimed that they actually cooked the
fish they caught in Yellowstone waters in an adjacent hot spring.
William Trumbull, a member of the Washburn expedition—which,
incidentally, included the famous campfire session where the idea
of a national park was reputedly suggested by Cornelius Hedges—
wrote an account of seeing a freshly caught trout boiled alive when
it flipped into a nearby hot spring:

> Several springs were in solid rock, within a few feet of the
> lake-shore. Some of them extended far out underneath the
> lake; with which, however, they had no connection. The
> lake water was quite cold, and that of these springs exceed-
> ingly hot. They were remarkably clear, and the eye could
> penetrate a hundred feet into their depths, which to the
> human vision appeared bottomless. A gentleman was fish-

ing from one of the narrow isthmuses, or shelves of rock, which divided one of these hot springs from the lake, when, in swinging a trout ashore, it accidentally got off the hook and fell into the spring. For a moment it darted about with wonderful rapidity, as if seeking an outlet. Then it came to the top, dead, and literally boiled. It died within a minute of the time it fell into the spring.

The Fishing Cone, situated on West Thumb at the bank of Yellowstone Lake, received its name from the repeated stunt of tourists hooking a trout in the lake's icy waters and then swinging it over to the steaming geyser to drop it in for a quick boil without ever taking it off the line. As the level of the lake rose over the last century, the water heating the geyser cooled to the point that it no longer erupts, and it's now considered a hot spring.

Fishing Cone wasn't the only place in Yellowstone where an angler could get a quick *sous-vide*. As Henry Winser reported in his 1883 book, *A Manual for Tourists*, the writer himself performed the feat several times in the Gardner River below the Mammoth Hot Springs terraces. Upon hooking a small trout on a fly, he would hoist it out of the cold water and swing it over to a boiling spring fifteen feet from the river, dropping the fish into the hot pot. "His life must have been extinguished instantly," he wrote, demonstrating a firm grasp of the obvious. All of the caught-and-cooked trout were sampled by the nine witnesses he'd assembled for the stunt. "It required from three to five minutes to thoroughly cook the victims of the experiment, and was the general verdict that they only needed a little salt to make them quite palatable."

Needless to say (we hope), the act of dropping a live trout into any of Yellowstone's thermal features is currently frowned upon.

When you turn on the tap in your kitchen sink, water just comes out. You don't have to think about the complex system of pipes and valves and pumps and heaters that make it possible for you to access a fresh water supply. It's the same with Old Faithful and the other towering geysers of Yellowstone. Their majesty and fearsome power continue to enthrall millions of visitors each year, most of whom are there to witness the end result of all that underground activity. Although it's fascinating, they don't need to know how it works. Old Faithful's wintertime eruptions have a beauty all their own, and many people swear that the coldest months are the best time to visit the park. The awesome force displayed by these boiling fountains belies the delicate and intricate workings that start far below the ground, and thankfully we're a lot better informed nowadays about taking care of these natural wonders. And, fortunately for both Old Faithful and those of us who may not have packed enough underwear, there are several clean, modern laundry facilities that can be found in Yellowstone Park at Lake Lodge, Old Faithful Snow Lodge, and Grant and Canyon Campgrounds, as well as the Fishing Bridge RV Park.

CHAPTER 12

Yancey's Ghost

There's nothing like overnighting in one of Yellowstone Park's historic rooms. Perhaps you've enjoyed the comforts of the recently remodeled Canyon Lodge, or maybe you've spent a few days headquartered at a cabin at the Old Faithful Snow Lodge, where you could watch the world's most famous geyser erupt without even getting out of your jammies. From the rustic Roosevelt Lodge Cabins to the historic Lake Yellowstone Hotel, our oldest national park offers more than two thousand rooms that will satisfy most levels of comfort. But when the morning sun slants in through the blinds and you throw back those covers to begin a new day of Yellowstone adventures, spend a few moments imagining what it must have been like for visitors in the early days of the park's existence. As on Gilligan's Island, it was "no phone, no lights, no motorcars, not a single luxury." Are you appreciating the sturdy wall between you and your neighbor who's entertaining his kids with his Yogi Bear impression? How about that nice hot shower to wash off the day's trail dust? After dealing with the no-ply toilet paper in the campground pit toilets, even a flushing commode seems like a godsend. However, the simplest amenities that we take for granted, even in the wilds of Yellowstone Park, were mere daydreams for a visitor during the park's first couple of decades.

One of the first pioneers to provide a measure of comfort for the fledgling park's weary travelers was "Uncle" John Yancey, a Kentuckian who, like many others, chased a fortune into the gold rush West. Yancey established an important mail station in the northern end of the park and built one of the very first hotels in Yellowstone. His five-room establishment, which he always referred to as "the ranch," served the miners, fishermen, teamsters, and soldiers traveling between Mammoth and Cooke City. Especially in the winter, the Pleasant Valley Hotel was a beacon in the night for cold, hungry, and tired travelers. Uncle John was a man who seemed larger than life—a proud, garrulous host who never tired of entertaining his guests with wild stories and tales of living in the park. The ten-acre parcel of land near the confluence of the Yellowstone and Lamar Rivers became synonymous with Uncle John, and it is still known as Yancey's Hole even though the last of the buildings was razed more than fifty years ago.

His hotel and saloon may be long gone, but can the same be said for Uncle John? Although he died in 1903, just days after attending the dedication of the Roosevelt Arch at Gardiner, many are convinced that his ghost remains in the Tower Junction area, bedeviling park employees and visitors at the Roosevelt Lodge for more than one hundred years. While his grave at Tinker's Cemetery in Gardiner contains his physical remains, is Uncle John's spirit still drifting around the northern end of the park that he loved so well?

Born in Barren County, Kentucky, in 1826, John Yancey was the sixth of ten children. While still a boy, he moved with his family to Missouri. He was twenty-three when the 1849 gold rush enticed so many young men to seek their fortune in the Wild West, and he joined the wave of opportunists moving to California. He later returned east to don a Confederate uniform and take up arms in the Civil War. After surviving America's bloodiest conflict, the prospect of gold still burned in Yancey's mind, leading him out West once again. A gold strike in the Crevice Creek area near the northern boundary of the newly created Yellowstone Park drew him to the rugged country just east of Mammoth, and by 1882 he'd had enough success as a prospector that he sold his portion of the Crevice Creek mining claim and was able to open a way station on the road between Gardiner and Cooke City. At age fifty-six, Uncle John was just getting started.

Park superintendent Patrick Conger gave Yancey verbal permission to establish a cabin in Pleasant Valley, where he could provide a room and provisions for stagecoach passengers traveling to and from the mining camps in Cooke City. In winter the road was the only route to the mining encampment. Sensing opportunity, Yancey built a cabin and mail station. Two years later his Pleasant Valley Hotel was also open for business. The rough-and-tumble log structure was thirty by fifty feet and stood one and a half stories tall. Its five austere rooms could sleep up to twenty guests, who paid the princely sum of $2 per day or $10 per week. Included in this fee were all meals, which were described as simple but generous in portion. Hotel guests dined on fresh trout, beef, cabbage, and other victuals obtained from the area. Fresh milk and cream were also available, courtesy of Yancey's small herd of cows.

Had TripAdvisor been around at the time, Yancey's rooms would probably have received a solid "any-port-in-a-storm" rating.

As it was, travel writers from the era routinely shared their disgust with the spartan accommodations, complaining of the horrific assault on their refined tastes. Like diners hoping to find a nice prime rib at a Burger King, these people missed the point entirely. Glamping, this was not.

"A visit to 'Uncle John Yancey's' ranch is an experience that will be remembered but which will not be repeated," sniffed world traveler Burton Holmes in his *Yellowstone Travelogue*. Like many who bunked at Yancey's expecting a certain level of cultivation or quality, Holmes was offended by the unvarnished amenities offered by Uncle John. For example, Yancey was quite proud of the "Kentucky Tea" he poured for his clientele. It was a fine whiskey called Kentucky Highstep, purchased in barrels. As noted in the accounts of Holmes and other visitors, Yancey always boasted that the glasses in which he served the libation had never been sullied with water (i.e., washed).

Hygiene was evidently not among Yancey's top concerns. Fortunately for hotel guests, responsibility for the upkeep and cleaning of the hotel, as well as the preparation of meals, fell to the women who worked for him. In 1887 a twenty-by-twenty-foot saloon was added to the hotel. This was the only aspect of the complex that fell completely under Yancey's purview, and it was consistently described as a pigsty. Marathon poker games, all-night bull sessions, and the occasional Kentucky Tea–fueled brawl were the order of the day in Yancey's saloon. Uncle John took to sleeping in a loft above the saloon, where one of his dogs would follow him right up the ladder to his bunk every night.

Yancey's Pleasant Valley Hotel, one of Yellowstone's earliest establishments. John Yancey is pictured on the fence in the foreground, with one of his ever-present dogs.

F. Jay Haynes, 1887. Haynes Foundation Collection, Montana Historical Society Research Center Photograph Archives, Helena, Montana.

There's a common equation among travelers and vacationers that holds true to this day—the acceptable level of quality for a night's accommodations drops inversely with the traveler's rising level of exhaustion. If you've just decided to call it a day after six hundred miles of back-wrecking, mind-numbing highway travel punctuated by greasy roadside meals and minivan backseat melees, that $49.95 two-bed flophouse room next to the railyard might seem like the Presidential Suite at the Plaza. But even after a day of rough and dusty stagecoach travel along the rugged road between Cooke City and Mammoth, many were still given pause by the seriously primitive conditions of the rooms inside Yancey's hotel.

When guests were ready to retire, they were given a small candle to light their way up the creaky stairway. The hallway, built of unfinished boards, stretched the length of the building, with the plank doors marked in chalk, designating rooms 1–5. You think the walls in that budget chain motel near the freeway were thin? The rooms at Yancey's were separated only by panels of cheesecloth, which also were used to create the ceiling. Gaps in the chinking of the log walls were plugged with wads of newspaper, and the glass in many of the small windows was broken. Each room was six feet by eight feet, the size of a typical modern jail cell. Next to the bed was a wooden box that supported a pitcher and bowl and a "crash towel." At this point, visitors probably gave up any hope of free ice. Each room sported a rug and was rounded out with a wooden chair for the guests' lounging comfort. The "bridal chamber" had additional luxury, which amounted to a four-by-six-inch mirror. As for clean sheets, well, visitors could only expect so much from the overworked chambermaid/cook/laundress. Reportedly a small bribe could persuade her to supply a guest with clean bed linens. Otherwise, as Carl E. Schmide wrote in 1910's *A Western Trip*, "The beds showed they were changed at least twice, once in the spring and once in the fall of the year."

So how did Uncle John Yancey, this rough pioneer who ran a shabby hotel and bucket-of-blood saloon, manage to become one of the most beloved characters in Yellowstone's history?

Yancey was "a peculiar sort of fellow—illiterate and rather certain of himself." So wrote Judge John Meldrum, Yellowstone's first US commissioner, about the grizzled old-timer who owned the Pleasant Valley Hotel. Judge Meldrum had a certain affection for the Kentucky frontiersman, and at one point Yancey's crude but forthright personality actually persuaded Meldrum to let him off the hook for a potential poaching infraction.

Yancey, like many settlers in the area, viewed the resources of Yellowstone as his for the taking and had a somewhat casual attitude toward park regulations. Although the park had created a set of rules and laws to abolish the illegal poaching of game by the time that Yancey built his hotel, enforcement of these laws was nearly impossible, as the US Army was pathetically short-handed for patrolling the 2.2-million-acre territory. So the miners, ranchers, hunters, and others who exploited the land routinely took loads of wood, hay, butchered game, and other bounty out of the park. Yancey, having received a lease from the government to run his business, was understandably discreet. He was reportedly a crack shot who could blast a chicken hawk out of the sky with his long rifle, and he always kept fresh elk and venison on the table for his guests. One day an army scout happened upon Yancey skinning a freshly killed elk. The scout reported the apparent infraction to Judge Meldrum, who issued a summons for Yancey to appear before him in Mammoth. Fully aware that it would be a two-day journey for Yancey from his home to Fort Yellowstone, Meldrum was not surprised when he received a note from Uncle John instead.

"Dear jedge," read the note, "You know I dan shoot no elk. I have a permit to shoot coyotes . . ." The note went on to explain Yancey's actions, which amounted to the elk being in the wrong place at the wrong time and falling victim to a bullet intended for a chicken-poaching coyote. Yancey had drilled the coyote, and when he went to retrieve the carcass he discovered the elk behind it. Thinking it a crime to let the meat go to waste, he was in the process of field dressing it when the scout came upon him.

The note, laboriously lettered in pencil and rife with the misspellings and grammatical errors of an uneducated woodsman, had the desired effect. Judge Meldrum, disarmed by Yancey's candor and backwoods charm, dismissed the case on the spot.

Yancey's rough life was plainly mapped in the crags of his face, and he looked like he might have been hewn from the rugged terrain of the park itself. In her 1897 article in the *Pittsburgh Press* titled "In the Yellowstone: Beauties of a Trip There in the Autumn," Mary Caldwell Ludwig describes Uncle John as "an odd character, whose looks encourage a belief in reincarnation, so forcibly does he remind us of the prehistoric." Yancey's rugged visage, combined with the compelling character of a raconteur, made him quite amusing to many of his guests. His peculiar appeal extended to the town of Gardiner, where he was well known and generally well liked. Many locals got a kick out of the quirky old hotel owner with the permanent squint and the billy-goat beard. Not everyone, however, was in love with the rustic charms of Yancey and his seedy hotel.

Acting superintendent John Pitcher saw the lack of refinement as potentially off-putting, perhaps even keeping people from visiting the park. He wrote in 1902 that the Pleasant Valley Hotel "is so wretched as to prevent many people from going to his place who [would] do so if he would furnish [them] with fairly decent fare." Still, Pitcher acknowledged that it was the shabbiness of the place that was attractive to a certain class of tourists who were looking for the authentic western experience. The hotel, he admitted, has "attractions, for a number of people, probably for the very reason of its roughness, and because it is a typical frontier establishment."

When President Theodore Roosevelt came to Gardiner to dedicate the entrance arch named after him in April 1903, Uncle John Yancey was there. He reportedly got the chance to meet the president after the ceremony, a momentary connection between two of the park's biggest supporters. Although April suggested spring on the calendar, it was still deep winter in Yellowstone. Yancey's two-day journey along the snowy roads to Mammoth proved to be too much for his health, and he reportedly caught a cold after arriving to witness the dedication of the arch. The cold degraded into full-blown pneumonia, and Yancey died in Gardiner two weeks later at the home of his friend C. B. Scott. He was seventy-seven.

Uncle John's funeral procession was the biggest the town had ever seen, a testament to the popularity of the old miner-turned-concessionaire. Most businesses closed for the day as people poured in from all over the area to join the procession and pay their respects. Yancey's obituary, published in the *Livingston Post*, was a veritable geyser of purple prose:

> One by one the frontiersmen who opened up the west to civilization are dropping away. . . . The last to answer the summons of the grim reaper was John Yancey, lovingly called Uncle John by all his acquaintances. The announcement of his demise carried grief and sorrow to the hearts of all who knew him. His rugged manhood, quick sympathy, broad charity, loving kindness and unswerving honor had endeared him to every person with whom he came in contact.

Yancey's nephew Dan took over the business upon his death, but tragedy struck again in 1906 when the hotel was destroyed by fire. The saloon, stable, and two other log structures survived, and in 1907 Dan applied for a lease to rebuild closer to the new road that was being constructed. By that time the Wylie Camping Company and the Yellowstone Park Association had a lock on new building permits in the area, and Dan's application was denied. His lease for the original site was revoked in November of that year. It wasn't until 1935 that Dan would receive $1,000 in compensation for the loss of his property. The saloon was bulldozed in the 1960s.

Hundreds of thousands of Yellowstone visitors pass through Yancey's Hole each year, near the foot of Crescent Hill just east of Mammoth. Xanterra Parks and Resorts hold stagecoach cookouts there on occasion, but by and large the history of Uncle John Yancey and his infamous hotel and saloon are fading away. That is, unless you believe the stories about Uncle John's mischievous ghost.

Park employees working at the Roosevelt Lodge have reported the sound of a tin cup being banged on the walls of the staff's quarters at 3:00 a.m. Objects disappear and then turn up in odd places with no explanation, they say. Out in the stables, horses have supposedly been unsaddled by some unseen presence, most often occurring with the horse of an attractive female rider. The legend of Yancey's ghost is one of the most persistent stories told in the park, as these odd experiences have been reported for more than a hundred years. If you're spending time in the north end of the park, perhaps traveling out to the Lamar Valley to observe the vast herds of Yellowstone bison, stop by the Roosevelt Lodge and raise a toast of Kentucky Tea to the memory of Uncle John Yancey, one of Yellowstone's most colorful characters. You might even receive a sign of approval from another realm if you drink it from an unwashed glass.

CHAPTER 13

Shipwreck on Yellowstone Lake

Anyone brave or crazy enough to take a canoe out onto Yellowstone Lake will tell you that a summer storm blowing through will raise waves big enough to swamp the *Titanic*. Most canoe and kayak enthusiasts stick to the western shores and the nonmotorized areas of the southern end of the lake. Hardier souls can opt for four- or six-day sea kayak tours around the lake, but storms come in quickly and even the most experienced skipper will be handing out life jackets when things turn hairy. The lake's most famous shipwreck, however, wasn't caused by turbulent waves or pummeling winds. The *E. C. Waters*, a massive 125-foot steamship, was sunk by the hubris and stubborn ambition of one of Yellowstone Park's most hated figures before it ever boarded a single paying passenger. The remains of the man's would-be salvation lie partially submerged at the shore's edge on Stevenson Island, a mile-long finger of land off the west shore of Yellowstone Lake's northern bulb. The unwanted craft had been abandoned in a cove of the island for years and eventually succumbed to the constant battering of ice, wind, and waves, with the smashed remains coming to rest near the shore. Having been stripped years earlier of its boiler and other usable parts, the carcass of the ship rests at a forty-five-degree angle at the waterline, wooden staves of the hull protruding from the sand like the ribs of a dinosaur. It serves as a stark reminder of the greed, reckless ambition, and cutthroat competition for tourist dollars that permeated Yellowstone as opportunistic businessmen wrestled for dominance in the wild and woolly early years of the world's original national park.

Yellowstone's first five years or so saw very few visitors, mostly hard-shelled locals who wanted to see for themselves the eye-popping wonders that had been reported by early explorers and organized expeditions and that led to President Grant's 1872 proclamation setting aside the area "for the enjoyment and benefit of the people." There were a few primitive roads cut through the mountainous terrain, but scarce amenities—a couple of tiny hotels here and there, serving food that was typically described as being fit for neither man nor beast. Travel was by horseback and, in winter, on ten-foot skis, propelled by a single long pole.

There was no real regulation in the park yet, and Wild West behavior abounded. Poaching, logging, prospecting, and other assaults on the park's abundant resources were widespread. It was time to call in the cavalry—literally. Company M of the US 1st Cavalry established a post at Mammoth Hot Springs in 1886 and took over management of the park. Captain Moses Harris was named the first acting superintendent of Yellowstone, and mounted troops roamed the expanse of the park, doing what they could to stem the vandalism to geysers and other destruction of the park's features.

At that time, post–Civil War America was shifting from an agricultural economy to an industrial one, and the money began to flow. East Coast gentry, bored with being underwhelmed by the puny adventure opportunities in their neck of the woods, turned their wealthy eyes to the West, where a wilderness wonderland held the promise of surreal natural features set in an untamed world still teeming with savages and monstrous mammals. Enter the Northern Pacific Railroad and its freshly laid tracks spanning thousands of miles. No dummies, the railroad bosses saw the opportunity to deliver the well-to-do to this new national park, separating them from some of their wealth along the way. Entrepreneurs and schemers converged on the park with similar visions of cashing in on this burgeoning business of high-end tourism. The Department of the Interior, which oversaw the newly created park, was inundated with requests for leases and permits to run touring companies, hotels, stores, and all manner of enterprises within Yellowstone's borders. One of these requests came from a man named Ela Collins Waters, a Civil War veteran and legislator for the Montana Territory. Waters had successfully run a couple of hotels in Montana, and when the Northern Pacific needed someone to oversee the five hotels it controlled in the park, Waters was their man.

Today's Yellowstone visitor might be appalled at some of the behavior displayed in the park by the well-heeled "dudes" pouring into the park by the thousands, delivered by train to Gardiner and West Yellowstone. From these gateway towns people were carried by stagecoach through the park, where they bathed in the hot pools of Mammoth's travertine terraces, carved their names into geyser cones, and threw all manner of junk into hot pools and geysers. The idea of preserving the fragile environment of this volcanic area was probably as far from their minds as establishing a colony on Mars.

The uniformed soldiers posted at the park's popular features did what they could to cut down on these incidents, but sometimes the very people leading tours were the ones crossing the line.

E. C. Waters was conducting one of these tours in the Old Faithful area in 1888. He poured soap into Beehive Geyser—a forbidden practice—to create a chemical reaction that would initiate an eruption. The geyser blew, the crowd cheered, and Waters was immediately arrested by soldiers patrolling the area. Captain Moses Harris, Yellowstone's first military superintendent, promptly ejected Waters and a few co-conspirators from the park. It was the second time that Harris had booted Waters from Yellowstone, and Waters's paranoia and compulsive opposition to authority were ignited in full. He somehow managed to keep his job and soon returned to Yellowstone, where his resentment toward both his overseers and his competitors continued to burn like a banked coal. It would fuel his behavior and color his judgment for the rest of his career, eventually leading to a shameful end, leaving him with a legacy as the most reviled man in the history of Yellowstone Park.

In the 1880s the twenty-mile overland journey by carriage or stagecoach from West Thumb to the newly constructed Lake Hotel on Yellowstone Lake's north shore was a dusty, bone-rattling excursion that sucked a lot of the fun out of many a vistor's vacation. Horses picked their way along the rutted trails at a mind-numbing crawl, and the ever-opportunistic Waters saw the chance to offer a seductive alternative. How about a nice, smooth boat ride across Yellowstone Lake, taking in the magnificent, snowcapped peaks in the distance and inhaling the bracing fragrance of pine forests ringing the lake? Sure beats choking on dust and trying to keep your joints from popping loose in a rattletrap stagecoach for three hours. Others had tried, and failed, to establish a waterborne tour of Yellowstone Lake. Now the Yellowstone Park Association (YPA), a thinly veiled enterprise of the all-powerful Northern Pacific Railroad, owned the rights to a boat tour business. That was enough to scare away a reasonable man, which was not an apt description of E. C. Waters. After a troublesome stint overseeing the construction of the Lake Hotel, Waters was caught up in a poaching scandal, fired by the YPA, and expelled, once again, from the park. Before the scandal, however, he'd already laid the groundwork for his own enterprise—the Yellowstone Lake Boat Company.

Waters slipped back into Yellowstone yet again, and after abandoning the idea of using naphtha-powered boats to ferry passengers, he thought back to his boyhood in Fond du Lac, Wisconsin, and the steamships he'd seen plying the waters of Lake Winnebago carrying freight and passengers. It was on Lake Minnetonka near Minneapolis that he would find his first boat. The YPA funded the purchase of the 120-passenger craft, a sad sack steamship that bore the name *Clyde*. Its three-foot draft was too deep to easily navigate the shallower sections of the lake, and when it hit its exhilarating top speed of sixteen miles per hour it tended to list to starboard. Around the Minnetonka docks it was known as *Useless*. Somehow Waters saw this as the perfect craft for his ambitious Yellowstone Lake venture.

The forty-ton boat was cut into three sections and transported nine hundred miles via railroad to Cinnabar. From there the sections were painstakingly loaded onto wagons for the arduous, sixty-mile trek through the park to the lake, involving a vertical climb of some three thousand feet. Once the sections were reunited at the lakeshore and the ship made seaworthy, the ever-shrewd Waters rechristened the steamship *Zillah*, presumably after the daughter of Northern Pacific president Thomas Oakes, one of the men who'd been arrested with Waters in the soapy scandal at Beehive Geyser. *Zillah* began carrying passengers, although Waters had not yet obtained a contract to operate from Interior Secretary John Noble. Still employed by the YPA, embroiled in the poaching scandal, and also facing charges of extortion from a meat contractor in the park, Waters pushed the YPA to its limit and was again fired. This time the sacking came directly from Oakes himself.

By now the *Zillah*, with its crew of seven, was fully operational. Despite the warnings from park superintendent Frazier Boutelle that he'd never get approval from Noble for his boat tour business, Waters did just that. He not only got a signed preliminary contract for operation on Yellowstone Lake but also secured leases for tracts of land along the lakeshore. Whether by luck, cunning, sheer force of will, or a combination of all three, Waters had succeeded in establishing a successful business on the shores of Yellowstone Lake. He also exacted a measure of revenge when, three weeks later, Boutelle was shown the door. Waters raised $100,000 in capital by selling stock in his boat enterprise, of which he bought 25 percent. The Yellowstone Lake Boat Company was afloat.

By this time the forty-year-old Waters spent each summer season in Yellowstone, living with his wife, two daughters, and a son in a house on the shore near the Lake Hotel. He'd already built a

Minnesota National Guard aboard the steamship *Zillah* at the West Thumb dock.
F. Jay Haynes. Haynes Foundation Collection, Montana Historical Society Research Center Photograph Archives, Helena, Montana.

reputation in the park as a shameless huckster and ruthless businessman, and complaints about his rude treatment of tourists flowed steadily into the office of the park superintendent. Waters was politically connected, however, having befriended Russell Harrison, the son of newly elected President Benjamin Harrison. Through constant political maneuvering and arm twisting (and allegedly bribing the young Harrison with $5,000 worth of stock), he tried to influence the Interior Department's policies on leasing within the park to favor his business ventures. He once proposed building an elevator that would carry passengers from the Yellowstone River in the park's Grand Canyon to the upper reaches of the canyon walls. That idea was, of course, rejected.

Waters felt the landscape shift beneath his feet (not literally, although this is Yellowstone) when the Panic of 1893 signaled the end of America's Gilded Age. The worst economic slump the country had ever seen translated to the smallest number of people to visit Yellowstone in ten years. Waters doubled down on Yellowstone's rebound, though, pouring money into a blacksmith service, a grocery store, several rowboats, and fishing gear to rent to his customers. He also sought leases for lakefront land where he could build boat landings around the lake, including a couple of islands. His request to lease land to build hotels was denied. It was his next harebrained proposal that would lead to the stubborn entrepreneur's biggest downfall and hasten his ouster from the park for good.

Waters looked at Yellowstone Lake's Dot Island and thought it would be the perfect place to build a zoo. Captive audiences aboard the *Zillah* could glide past the island and get up close and personal with bison, elk, bighorn sheep, and other "exotic" animals that would roam the island in a natural setting. He laid out his proposal in a two-page, handwritten letter to acting superintendent George Anderson, Captain Boutelle's successor. Anderson, well aware that the bison's numbers had dwindled from the untold millions that roamed the West just a few decades earlier to the couple of hundred that remained in the park, approved the plan with the stipulation that the bison would have to come from outside the park. Waters had this requirement covered and purchased four bison from the famed Goodnight Herd in Texas. Pens were constructed on Dot Island, and soon elk, bison, and several bighorn sheep were wandering the long strip of land, thrilling *Zillah* passengers whose exorbitant $2.50 fee included a close pass by the island. Each fall, at the end of tourist season, the zoo would close and a barge carrying the stock would take the animals to pens near the Lake Hotel, where they wintered.

But, Waters being Waters, it wasn't enough. He proposed putting several Indians and a couple of tepees on the island to further replicate the "natural" setting that suggested the unspoiled West. Incredibly, this repugnant idea was approved by the secretary of the interior and the commissioner of Indian affairs, as long as the Native Americans participated willingly and were reimbursed for travel expenses. Fortunately, the plan never came to fruition.

By 1890 the *Zillah* was ferrying loads of passengers up the northwest side of Yellowstone Lake, creating a nice little income stream for Waters. Still, he wondered why business wasn't as brisk as it should have been. He found out why when he learned that YPA employees, from stagecoach drivers to tour guides, had been badmouthing his boat company and zoo to the park's tourists. Waters quickly countered by offering a fifty-cent kickback to every stagecoach driver who steered a paying customer his way. He also printed up handbills that were distributed aboard the trains running the spur lines off the main Northern Pacific into the park's entrance communities.

Aside from his constant harangue aimed at pretty much every tourist who crossed his path, Waters continued to run afoul of park officials with his sordid behavior. He was arrested for driving his horse-drawn cart at night without permission near Natural Bridge, where it was said that he took his occasional tryst partners. He was also chastised for cutting wood and hay without authorization. In addition to the complaints rolling in through normal channels, the Yellowstone grapevine was buzzing about Waters and his misdeeds: He insulted women. He overcharged customers. He lied to rowboat renters about giving a full refund if they didn't catch any fish. Not only that, but he also constantly disparaged every other transportation company in the park.

A special investigation launched by the Interior Department found that, among other transgressions, Waters was keeping a veritable stock farm, which included twenty cows, thirty horses, and fifty to seventy sheep, as well as several hogs and chickens, penned up less than fifty feet from the Lake Hotel. With the hotel embarking on a massive renovation, officials wanted Waters out. They also knew that he was as stubborn as a tick, so they recommended that a competing boat company be encouraged to operate on the lake. Waters would have to either clean up his act (highly unlikely) or throw in the towel. In typical Waters fashion, he ignored the report and attacked its source, launching a campaign to have then–acting superintendent John Pitcher ousted from Yellowstone.

Meanwhile, Harry Child, who had operated a successful stagecoach company, managed to buy the YPA (with the help of some railroad financing), something Waters had sought and failed to do. Child agreed to promote Waters's boat business if he would take down all the decrepit buildings he'd constructed in the area near the Lake Hotel. Their tenuous truce dissolved when Waters blew up at Child over a perceived slight. Child, who had been in Helena during the episode Waters was railing about, sent a letter to

Superintendent Pitcher recommending that they cut all ties with Waters. Pitcher in turn contacted the secretary of the interior and urged him to kick Waters out of Yellowstone once and for all. "In one way or another he has been the source of almost every complaint that has come into your office," he wrote.

By this time William H. Wylie had begun to make inroads into the park with his camping business. The distinctive Wylie Camping Co. blue-and-white-striped tents sprouted throughout the park, offering a more affordable way for the hoi polloi to enjoy the attractions of "Wonderland." Wylie could have been a powerful ally in Waters's battle with the park powers, but the boatman's petty nature and insufferable self-importance repelled Wylie.

Like a bison walking into a blizzard, Waters bulled ahead. His paranoia drove him to collect affidavits from everyone he could get to swear that the YPA (now the Yellowstone Park Hotel Company) had conspired against him. He bound these affidavits into a booklet and somehow got it into the hands of New York's governor, Benjamin B. Odell, who wrote to President Theodore Roosevelt to ask for some intervention. Waters also raked Yellowstone's Superintendent Pitcher over the coals for allowing alcohol to be served at park hotels, causing all manner of wild behavior. But Roosevelt and Pitcher were good friends, and the president was already well aware of the deeds and reputation of the blowhard businessman from Yellowstone who had taken to calling himself "Captain" Waters.

During Waters's escalating battle with park officials and the government, word reached the press that Waters was having a new steamship built, a seven-hundred-passenger behemoth that would replace the *Zillah*. The *Minneapolis Journal* reported that the steamship "would be the finest craft afloat between the Great Lakes and the Puget Sound." Waters, as usual, was digging in for a long battle by putting everything he had on the line. He had no way of knowing that his empire and his life would begin to unravel that winter.

In January 1905, his eighteen-year-old daughter, Anna, committed suicide in the family's Fond du Lac home. She had been suffering from depression and ended it by drinking a bottle of chloroform. Waters was, of course, devastated, but a letter he drafted a week later exemplified the man's self-absorption. He couldn't even acknowledge his daughter's untimely death without making it about himself. She had been saddened, he wrote, at her father's mistreatment at the hands of park officials, and the damage to his business was what must have driven her to end her own life.

The following summer saw Yellowstone's biggest year. The centennial of the Lewis and Clark Expedition in 1906 helped boost the number of park visitors to twenty-six thousand people, an all-time high. While the feud between Waters and, well, everyone else continued to boil, the parts for his new steamship began to arrive at the lake. A temporary shipyard was built at Yellowstone Lake's edge, and a team of skilled shipwrights quickly assembled the humongous craft. By summer's end, it was ready to be christened. Still in need of fitting out with the final details, the steamship was launched at a ceremony attended by hundreds of people. Captain Waters, now fifty-six, had survived for twenty years in the park, fending off rivals—both real and imagined—at every turn. He had his daughter Edna crack a bottle of champagne across the boat's bow while his wife looked on. It was christened, of course, the *E. C. Waters*.

A new wrinkle now affected Waters's shaky future: His ten-year lease for the boat business was about to expire. Superintendent Pitcher, Waters's longtime nemesis, used the situation to suggest to the secretary of the interior that a new boat company be installed to help mitigate the losses from a steep drop in tourist numbers following the centennial year. The Wylie Camping Co., he wrote, might be interested. Meanwhile, the *E. C. Waters* remained moored on the east side of Stevenson Island, having yet to carry its first paying passenger. Waters learned from an inside source that the railroad-controlled park concession conglomerate was indeed trying to take control of his business in order to tie up all of the park's enterprises. He found yet another highly placed official, a New York congressman, to intercede on his behalf. Waters was granted a one-year lease but given no provisions to buy him out after the season. He knew that he was on his way out the door, and all his money, as well as a hefty inheritance his wife had received, was tied up in the boat company and its assets.

While Waters awaited a buyer for the *Zillah*, his rowboats and gear, grocery story, blacksmith shop, animals, and of course the still-dormant *E. C. Waters*, complaints started to pour in from tourists about the abominable conditions faced by the bison and elk at his "zoo" on Dot Island. Waters, who had fallen ill and was in a tuberculosis sanitarium in Fond du Lac, blamed the government. Once he had regained his health, he returned to the park in June 1907. By then, however, Pitcher and his successor Samuel Young had built a case against Waters, and soon game wardens visited the island and were horrified by the squalor and filth in which the emaciated animals were forced to live, in full view of several thousand tourists passing by the island aboard the *Zillah* each summer.

The zoo was shut down immediately, Waters's pens near the hotel were torn down, and all the animals were turned loose to run free in the park. Waters left Yellowstone in September, and a bulletin was issued by Superintendent Young that he was banned from the park, "having rendered himself obnoxious during the season of 1907."

It was over. Waters's only chance to have anything to show for his twenty-year run in Yellowstone was finding a buyer for his boats and equipment. He set the price for the business at $300,000—$200,000 for assets and $100,000 for the "goodwill" he'd built up over the years. He had one offer but was unable to secure the promise of a ten-year lease that the buyer wanted. Ex-guide Billy Hofer started a new boat operation with ten motorboats and fifty rowboats. Nobody wanted the steamships.

Waters never returned to the park again. His health deteriorated until he wound up in a Wisconsin veterans home, where he slowly went insane. After a long illness, he died at age seventy-seven.

It's unknown what became of the *Zillah*, the rust bucket that had been Waters's workhorse for sixteen years. One theory is that it was towed out into the open water of the four-hundred-foot-deep lake and scuttled. As for the *E. C. Waters*, it remained for several years, abandoned, anchored in an inlet on Stevenson Island. Eventually the wind, waves, and ice coming off the lake pummeled the craft up onto the beach of the island. Crews picked it clean of salvage, including the huge iron boiler, which was used to heat the Lake Hotel for forty-six years. The remaining hulk sat at the edge of the island, where it was visited in the winter by adventurers and partyers willing to cross the expanse of ice to the island. In 1931 two park rangers and a caretaker skied out to the wreck, doused the eyesore with kerosene, and set it ablaze.

The *E. C. Waters* proved to be as stubborn as its namesake, however. Only a small part of the wreckage burned, and soon after the attempted immolation park officials realized that the remaining hulk represented an important part of Yellowstone's story. So it remains today, viewable by visitors on tour boats and watercraft, the forlorn wreckage that bears witness to the park's early days and the long, checkered career of one man whose own tenacious and vile nature somehow allowed him to thrive while becoming one of the most loathed men in the history of Yellowstone Park.

CHAPTER 14

Obsidian Cliff

Reports began to work their way back East in the early 1800s. Trappers and mountain men operating around the Continental Divide south of the Lewis and Clark trail sent word about a fantastic land they'd encountered: a place where water and clay shot skyward from the earth, colorful hot pools by the dozens steamed the air with sulfurous clouds, and the earth itself rumbled like thunder. Many of these descriptions were dismissed as the wild exaggerations of men who'd spent a little too long in the oxygen-starved air of the northern Rocky Mountains. But after John Colter first skirted the eastern edge of the Yellowstone plateau in the winter of 1807–1808, explorers began working their way through the area to trap beavers for the trading posts that were proliferating in the Mountain West. Men like Osborne Russell, David Folsom, Jim Bridger, and others wrote accounts of Yellowstone's incredible features and shocking hydrothermal activity. Colter's legend is well known, and he is widely considered the first white man to set foot in Yellowstone, but evidence abounds that he was pretty late to the party.

So who beat the mountain men to Yellowstone? Many of the explorers of European descent dismissed the idea that Indians were ever in the area. The commonly accepted theory during the time of western expansion was that Indians were terrified of the Yellowstone region and avoided the place for fear of the angry gods that inhabited the plateau in the form of geysers, steam vents, and other geothermal features. While this ignorant attitude was actually embraced by many who hoped to exploit the land and promote the national park, recent archaeological discoveries such as petroglyphs and artifacts from the area have shown that not only did Indians have no such fear of the Yellowstone region, but they also had been moving through the mystical plateau for thousands of years. As many as two dozen western tribes spent time in Yellowstone, and many of them were drawn there by one very big resource: a massive deposit of obsidian, the biggest in North America. Fragments of the glossy black stone featuring the unique chemical signature of the volcanic glass of Yellowstone's Obsidian Cliff have been found as far away as Maine and Central America, and it's been estimated that the huge lithic deposit has been an important source of obsidian for tools and weapons for North America's human residents for as long as twelve thousand years. While early explorers theorized that the reclusive Tukudeka, or Sheepeaters, were the only Indians to inhabit Yellowstone, arriving sometime in the 1700s, the 3,580-acre hunk of cooled rhyolite lava known as Obsidian Cliff says otherwise. When it comes to "discovering" Yellowstone, John Colter wasn't even close to first.

As you're driving on Yellowstone's Grand Loop Road between Norris and Mammoth, you'll pass Beaver Lake, a large, marshy pond on the west side of the road about thirteen miles south of Mammoth. If you're scanning the wetlands for moose or bear, you just might miss one of Yellowstone's most glorious and historically significant features. Known as Glass Mountain until the park's second superintendent, Philetus Norris, bestowed its more geologically accurate name in 1873, Obsidian Cliff looms over the east side of the road, towering 150–200 feet above Obsidian Creek. Up near the top of the half-mile-long promontory, a broad, horizontal band of gleaming black obsidian, streaked with yellow and red, is plainly visible from the road. When the sun's out, it positively sparkles. You're looking at the largest deposit of obsidian in North America. Strewn around the base of the cliff are thousands of obsidian rocks and boulders, some as big as a trash can. While it's illegal to remove any obsidian from the park, these fragments can be examined. Be careful, though—sifting through a pile of obsidian flakes can be like running your hand through a bunch of razor blades. Obsidian's appeal is its extreme sharpness. Indians knapped it to a fine edge for projectile points, knives, and tools, and even today some surgeons prefer to use obsidian-tipped scalpels for eye surgery and heart bypass operations, as the edge is sharper than any surgical steel. An obsidian edge can actually cut on a cellular level.

Obsidian Cliff is one of four volcanic flows north of the Yellowstone caldera, part of the Roaring Mountain Member of the Rhyolite Plateau that formed about 183,000 years ago. As the lava cooled and crystallized, the cracks formed the vertical columns of the cliffs. The black, glass-like deposit of obsidian was the result of the lava cooling rapidly without crystallizing. The visible black strata in the cliff are nearly one hundred feet wide in places, and the obsidian is most abundant at ground level. The color of the spherulitic rock varies with the type and level of impurities it contains, running from charcoal black to brown, red, green, and mottled patterns.

Yellowstone's first visitors likely began their movement up the Asian Pacific coast toward the end of the Ice Age about forty thousand years ago. A couple million years of glacial cycles had scoured out valleys, piled up continental plates, covered huge parts of the earth in ice sheets, and eaten away at Mount Kenya, Mount Kilimanjaro, and other monoliths. Species came and went as the cycles of cooling and warming destroyed or created habitat for constantly evolving life. Ancestors of modern humans, who originated in Africa, likely worked their way east across the Beringia land bridge between North America and northeast Asia. As global cooling lowered water levels and exposed more land, the terra firma between the continents allowed small populations of humans to flow across the land bridge around twelve thousand years ago and fan out across North America. In addition, archaeological sites recently found in North America pre-date the time of the Beringia theory, suggesting that coastal sea travel may have been another avenue to the continent. It's also thought that many of these groups were hunter-gatherers who were following mammals such as mastodons as they migrated into the new area. The Yellowstone River drainage had been formed some time earlier, near the end of the Pleistocene Glaciation, the last ice age.

In 1959, in Gardiner, Montana, Otho Mack was on the construction site of a new post office just a few miles north of Yellowstone Park. From the excavated material he plucked a small piece of stone that caught his eye. He identified it as the heel of an obsidian projectile point. He contacted the University of Colorado Museum, and the curator of anthropology, Joe Ben Wheat, confirmed that the fragment was definitely part of a Clovis Point. Named after the New Mexico city where examples were first found in 1929, the distinctive projectile points are thought to have been used by a highly mobile culture that followed the roaming megafauna like lions and mammoths in the late Pleistocene. The design is unique to North America, and the discovery of the Clovis fragment in Gardiner was a strong indication that the first human visitors to Yellowstone were in the area at least eleven thousand years ago. Other projectile points of different types had been found in the park, mostly at higher elevations, as early as 1900. The Clovis Point, however, suggested that these other, lanceolate points were indicators that early hunters had been in the area after the Great Extinction of six thousand years ago wiped out many species and made the area largely uninhabitable by humans.

With their food source eradicated, early hunters also disappeared, eventually to be replaced by post–Ice Age foragers who lived on nuts, berries, roots, seeds, and whatever fish or birds they could capture. As the modern fauna returned to the area, they also became hunters, using a leverage device called an atlatl to throw a short spear tipped with an obsidian point.

As climatic severity made travel more difficult, foragers began to inhabit smaller areas, moving back and forth to the least inhospitable terrain during the seasonal changes. In summer the Indians moved to the higher hunting grounds of the mountains, where bighorn sheep and elk were plentiful, and in winter they moved into the lower elevations of the valleys where bison congregated. These Indians would eventually be identified as the Tukudeka, a subset of the Shoshone. The Sheepeaters, as they were called, are the only tribe known to inhabit Yellowstone year-round. However, despite the claims of nineteenth-century explorers, these Mountain Shoshone weren't the only Indians to frequent the area. As many as two dozen western tribes came into Yellowstone for thousands of years, right up until the tragic Indian Wars of the late 1800s. Most of these tribes shared a common resource: obsidian. Although there's little hard evidence to back it up, oral histories have suggested that Obsidian Cliff existed as a kind of DMZ, a sacred place where scrapping between tribes was not allowed. The lithic material was so important to the Indians' existence that all tribes came to the cliffs unmolested and collected rough material to be worked elsewhere. When warlike tribes like the Sioux and the Comanche could set aside their differences long enough to retrieve this vital element of their existence, it's clear that the importance of Obsidian Cliff to the Indian culture can't be overstated.

So how did the shaped points from Obsidian Cliff make it as far away as Ohio and Canada? Indian trading networks is one answer. Paleo-Indians traded copper from the upper Great Lakes, shells from the Gulf of Mexico, mica from the Carolinas, and obsidian from Obsidian Cliff, among other things. Hopewell Indian sites in Ohio yielded not only spear points and knives made from Yellowstone material but also a 660-pound cache of raw obsidian that came from the Obsidian Cliff deposit. A technique called obsidian hydration dating has identified far-flung pieces of obsidian as having come from the Yellowstone site ten thousand years ago.

Another answer to the question of the wide dispersal of Yellowstone obsidian among tribes is horses. Spanish and Mexican explorers

Obsidian Cliff, from which dozens of Indian tribes have sourced the crucial stone for more than twelve thousand years.

Ednor Therriault.

were trade partners with the Indians in the 1800s, and it was the Spanish who introduced the horse to the Indian culture via the Utes. As the animals were bred and their use spread across the plains, the horse drastically changed the lifestyles of many tribes as they shifted from a hunter-gatherer lifestyle to a more nomadic one due to their new, four-legged means of transportation. Hunters and warriors traveled farther and faster, and each tribe's culture spread farther into the surrounding territory. Obsidian arrowheads and other projectile points were thus spread far and wide in all directions. Indians even traded a few arrowheads to their fur-trading partners, but these were usually metal points they'd crafted in the post-gun era.

Free trade is a misnomer, as we've learned, and the US government enacted legislation to regulate trade with the Indians by passing the Trade and Intercourse Act in 1790. The Indian Office, then part of the War Department, later issued licenses to traders in Indian Territory. The Constitution itself actually contains a clause giving the United States the power to "regulate Commerce with foreign Nations, and among the several States, and with the Indian tribes." As the nineteenth century wore on, the United States used the power it had given itself to nullify the tribes' claims to their homeland so they could be moved to reservations.

While the trading post is an extinct relic from an earlier time of cooperation and mutual benefit, many of today's tribal members are keeping their heritage alive by passing down their native languages and cultural traditions to younger generations. Among these traditions is the primitive skill of knapping, the shaping of a rough obsidian slab into a sleek and effective projectile point, knife, or scraping tool. It's a process that's been used for thousands of years and still has its enthusiasts today. The by-products of lithic reduction have provided anthropologists with an invaluable tool by which to ascribe age, identity, and other clues into the source of many archaeological sites.

Knapping, to put it simply, involves breaking open a piece of parent material and choosing one of the flakes to work into the desired shape. Percussion flaking is the technique of using a tool made of antler or bone to strike the stone material at an angle. Obsidian is the most prized of lithic materials because it is fine grained and isotropic, meaning that it has the same molecular structure in all directions. It breaks off cleanly and predictably. When working with obsidian the danger level is pretty high, as the edges of these translucent flakes that fly off the obsidian nodule can be as thin as a couple of molecules. Today's knappers wear eye protection, but one has to wonder why there weren't huge numbers of blinded Indian craftsmen stumbling around the West.

The stone is worked on the knapper's lap, which is covered with a protective material like rawhide or leather. To break the material cleanly, the craftsman strikes sharply at the surface with his tool—percussive pressure—and the resulting break will typically crack the stone in a wedge shape, which is called a Hertzian cone. The angle of the break is usually about one hundred degrees wide. An understanding of how force moves through stone allows the craftsman to make controlled breaks of the material, slowly achieving the desired shape.

The fine-tuned shaping process is called pressure flaking. This stage is when the knapper uses the sharp end of an antler or other tool to press against an edge of the biface, popping off a long, thin flake. Careful pressure flaking allows the knapper to gradually reduce the biface to the desired shape, biface meaning that both sides of the piece are worked (bifacial). Projectile points such as arrowheads need to be hafted onto a shaft, typically with rawhide or sinew, so notches at the lower corners must be worked into the point. For fine work such as this, a small, abrasive tool is used in conjunction with pressure flaking to create the notch.

John Colter and his early Yellowstone contemporaries probably passed right by many reduction sites in and around the park as they tromped around the Northern Rockies, completely unaware that these scattered piles of obsidian flakes, or debitage, were left by Indians who'd brought the materials from Obsidian Cliff hundreds or thousands of years earlier. Reduction sites are scattered throughout the West, and the presence of obsidian where there is no natural obsidian source points to a spot where Indians would set up camp and reduce the large pieces of rock they'd carried from elsewhere into smaller pieces (or preform bifaces) that could be fine-tuned later, in a safer or more comfortable environment. The morphology, size, and shape of the debitage can be another clue to the tribal identities of these early knappers. Other techniques like debitage refitting (like putting together a puzzle) can indicate the type of tool used, or perhaps what the maker was creating. Analysis of the debitage can also be used to source and date the material.

Even with these advanced processes, sometimes the answers to the mysteries hidden in a reduction site can't be fully investigated. When is an arrowhead not an arrowhead? While hikers and arrowhead hunters turn up obsidian points all over the United States, only a few of these are actual arrowheads. Many of the pieces are knives, scrapers, drills, spear points, or other items intended for a specific use by their original creator. Additionally, a small arrowhead or dart point may have started its life as a scraper or knife. Many amateur archaeologists who find a larger, point-shaped piece assume that it's a blank that was meant to be worked down to a small projectile point. In reality, most Indians wanted to get the most bang for their buck from a nice hunk of obsidian. What started out as a hide scraper may have been used for a while and, when it became dull, knapped down to a knife or other tool. That, in turn, could be reduced to a spear point or drill. By the time an obsidian piece was flaked down to a small dart point, it may already have gone through many incarnations as a useful tool or weapon.

When Philetus Norris realized the geological significance of the shiny black cliff a few miles north of the hot springs that now bear his name, he (perhaps unknowingly) took the first step toward debunking the myth of John Colter's "discovery" of Yellowstone Park. As crews began work on improving the trail that would eventually become part of the Grand Loop Road, he allowed the construction crew to use materials sourced from the area for their project. He also instructed them to keep an eye open for any artifacts they might come across. Workers built fires atop the blocks of slick black rock, and when they became heated, they threw cold water on them, causing them to fracture. Using this abundant raw material, they built the world's only glass road.

In 1931 the park constructed a roadside kiosk, a cozy pull-out meant to provide visitors with a break from the road as well as information about Obsidian Cliff. The first such installation in the park, it was built in the National Park Service rustic style and was soon joined by other interpretive exhibits along the Grand Loop Road. The stone and wood structure houses a couple of informational panels that tell some of the story of Obsidian Cliff, both historical and geological. But as we continue to learn more about Paleo-Indian culture and the important role played by Yellowstone's stunning mass of volcanic glass, Obsidian Cliff will be telling the story at its own pace.

BIBLIOGRAPHY

YELLOWSTONE'S CAMPFIRE ORIGIN MYTH

"Birth of a National Park." Yellowstone National Park, National Park Service, U.S. Department of the Interior. www.nps.gov/ yell/learn/historyculture/yellowstoneestablishment.htm.

Chittenden, Hiram Martin. *The Yellowstone National Park: Historical and Descriptive*. London: Forgotten Books, 2016.

"Cornelius Hedges Family Papers, 1828–1945." Archives West, 2005. archiveswest.orbiscascade.org/ark:/80444/xv63617.

Haines, Aubrey L. *The Yellowstone Story: A History of Our First National Park*. Yellowstone Association for Natural Science, History & Education, 1996.

Magoc, Chris J. *Yellowstone: The Creation and Selling of an American Landscape, 1870–1903*. Albuquerque: University of New Mexico Press, 1999.

Merrill, Marlene Deahl, ed. *Yellowstone and the Great West: Journals, Letters, and Images from the 1871 Hayden Expedition*. Lincoln: University of Nebraska Press, 2003.

Schullery, Paul, and Lee H. Whittlesey. *Myth and History in the Creation of Yellowstone National Park*. Lincoln: University of Nebraska Press, 2003.

OLD SNAGGLETOOTH

"Aged Bear Is Killed." *Havre Daily News*, June 26, 1970. www.
newspapers.com/image/11975583/?terms=Old%2B
Snaggletooth.

"Bear Management." Yellowstone National Park, National Park
Service, U.S. Department of the Interior. www.nps.gov/yell/
learn/nature/bearmgmt.htm.

Giaimo, Cara. "Yellowstone Owes Its Early Success to Public Bear
Feeding." *Atlas Obscura*, August 31, 2016. www.atlasobscura
.com/articles/yellowstone-owes-its-early-success-to-public
-bear-feeding.

"No More Lunch Counter for Yellowstone Bears." *My Yellowstone
Park*, June 21, 2011. www.yellowstonepark.com/things-to-do/
yellowstone-bears-no-longer-get-garbage-treats.

Reichard, Sean. "Yellowstone History: Bear Feeding." *Yellowstone
Insider*, July 11, 2016. https://yellowstoneinsider
.com/2016/07/11/yellowstone-history-bear-feeding/.

Whittlesey, Lee H. *Death in Yellowstone: Accidents and
Foolhardiness in the First National Park*. Lanham, MD: Roberts
Rinehart, an imprint of Rowman & Littlefield, 2014.

LEGEND OF THE SHEEPEATERS

Janetski, Joel C. *The Indians of Yellowstone Park*. Salt Lake City:
University of Utah Press, 1987.

Loendorf, Lawrence L., et al. *Mountain Spirit: The Sheepeater Indians of Yellowstone*. Salt Lake City: University of Utah Press, 2006.

"Mummy Cave." *Wikipedia*. https://en.wikipedia.org/wiki/Mummy_Cave.

Taylor, Beth. "Inside Yellowstone—Sheepeater Cliff." Yellowstone National Park, National Park Service, U.S. Department of the Interior, April 27, 2007. www.nps.gov/yell/learn/photosmultimedia/0006sheepeater-cliff-iy.htm.

"Tukudeka." *Wikipedia*. https://en.wikipedia.org/wiki/Tukudeka.

Vestal, Stanley. *Jim Bridger, Mountain Man: A Biography*. Lincoln: University of Nebraska Press, 1970.

YELLOWSTONE LAKE'S MYSTERIOUS MUSIC

"High Frequency Active Auroral Research Program." *Wikipedia*. https://en.wikipedia.org/wiki/High_Frequency_Active_Auroral_Research_Program.

"Mysterious Sounds Like Whispers on Lake Yellowstone." *My Yellowstone Park*, September 27, 2013. www.yellowstonepark.com/things-to-do/yellowstone-mysterious-lake-music.

Prevost, Ruffin. "Yellowstone 'Lake Music' Remains Mystery a Century after Written Reports." *Yellowstone Gate*, February 23, 2012. www.yellowstonegate.com/2012/02/no-explanation-for-mysterious-lake-music-reported-by-many-yellowstone-visitors/.

Spencer, Janet. *Yellowstone Trivia: Including Crossword Puzzles, Quote Quests, Word Games & More*. Helena, MT: Riverbend Publishing, 2006.

Whittlesey, Lee H. *Death in Yellowstone: Accidents and Foolhardiness in the First National Park*. Lanham, MD: Roberts Rinehart, an imprint of Rowman & Littlefield, 2014.

"Why Do Corpses Sunk in Water Eventually Float to the Surface?" *My Q/A Corner*. http://myqacorner.blogspot.com/2012/01/why-do-corpses-sunk-in-water-eventually_01.html.

"Yellowstone's Whispering Lake." Travel Channel. www.travel channel.com/videos/yellowstones-whispering-lake-0171284.

THE DEVIL'S KITCHENETTE

Haines, Aubrey L. *The Yellowstone Story: A History of Our First National Park*. Yellowstone Association for Natural Science, History & Education, 1996.

Rafferty, Shae. "Suffragettes in Yellowstone 3: The Trischman Family." Yellowstone National Park, National Park Service, U.S. Department of the Interior, August 14, 2014. www.nps.gov/yell/blogs/suffragettes-in-yellowstone-3-the-trischman-family.htm.

Watry, Elizabeth A. "Anna K. Trischman Pryor and Elizabeth 'Belle' Trischman." In *Women in Wonderland: Lives, Legends and Legacies of Yellowstone National Park*, 37–60. Helena, MT: Riverbend Publishing, 2012.

THE GHOSTS OF OLD FAITHFUL INN

"Ghost Stories Give Old Faithful Inn a Haunting Reputation." *Deseret News*, July 4, 1991. www.deseretnews.com/article/ 170908/GHOST-STORIES-GIVE-OLD-FAITHFUL-INN -A-HAUNTING-REPUTATION.html?pg=all.

"Ghosts of Yellowstone." *My Yellowstone Park*, October 31, 2013. www.yellowstonepark.com/park/ghosts-of-yellowstone.

Schlosser, S. E. "The Headless Bride." In *Spooky Yellowstone: Tales of Hauntings, Strange Happenings, and Other Local Lore*, 21–27. Guilford, CT: Globe Pequot Press, 2013.

Scofield, Susan C., and Jeremy Schmidt. *The Inn at Old Faithful: The Last Word in Hotel Building, a Virtual Leviathan of Log Cabin Construction Located in Our Great National Park Yellowstone*. Crowsnest Associates, 1979.

Spencer, Janet. *Yellowstone Trivia: Including Crossword Puzzles, Quote Quests, Word Games & More*. Helena, MT: Riverbend Publishing, 2006.

THE ZONE OF DEATH

Baynham, Jacob. "There's a Section of Yellowstone Where You Can Get Away with Murder." *Vice Guided Tours*, August 4, 2016. www.vice.com/en_us/article/zn8nnw/theres-a-50 -square-mile-section-of-yellowstone-where-you-can-get -away-with-murder.

Box, C. J. *Free Fire*. New York City: G. P. Putnam's Sons, 2016.

Kalt, Brian C. "The Perfect Crime." *Georgetown Law Journal* 93, no. 2 (March 25, 2005): 1–23. https://papers.ssrn.com/sol3/papers.cfm?abstract_id=691642.

Rossen, Jake. "The Perfect Crime May Be Possible in Yellowstone Park." *Mental Floss*, July 20, 2016. http://mentalfloss.com/article/83439/perfect-crime-may-be-possible-yellowstone-park.

Schweber, Nate. *Fly Fishing Yellowstone National Park: An Insider's Guide to the 50 Best Places.* Mechanicsburg, PA: Stackpole/Headwater Books, 2012.

BIGFOOT IN YELLOWSTONE?

"Bigfoot Reports in Wyoming." *Reports for Wyoming*, Bigfoot Field Researchers Organization. www.bfro.net/GDB/state_listing.asp?state=wy.

"'Bigfoot' Spotted in Yellowstone National Park?" *National Geographic*, February 10, 2015. https://news.national geographic.com/news/2015/02/150210-bigfoot-science -animals-yellowstone-Sasquatch-myths-culture/.

Stein, T. E. "Yellowstone Backcountry Ranger Describes Sighting, Other Incidents." Bigfoot Field Researchers Organization, August 12, 2005. www.bfro.net/gdb/show_report.asp?id =12302.

HOW ONE ARREST SAVED YELLOWSTONE'S BUFFALO

"Charles 'Buffalo' Jones." *Wikipedia.* https://en.wikipedia.org/wiki/Charles_%22Buffalo%22_Jones.

Gates, Charles Cormack, and Len Broberg. *Yellowstone Bison: The Science and Management of a Migratory Wildlife Population.* Missoula: University of Montana Press, 2011.

Hough, Emerson, et al. *Rough Trip through Yellowstone: The Epic 1894 Winter Expedition of Emerson Hough, F. Jay Haynes, and Billy Hofer: Including the Capture of Notorious Buffalo Poacher Ed Howell.* Helena, MT: Riverbend Publishing, 2013.

Krech, Shepard. "Buffalo Tales: The Near-Extermination of the American Bison." *Native Americans and the Land,* National Humanities Center, July 2001. http://nationalhumanitiescenter .org/tserve/nattrans/ntecoindian/essays/buffalo.htm.

"Lacey Act of 1900." *Wikipedia.* https://en.wikipedia.org/wiki/ Lacey_Act_of_1900.

Spencer, Janet. *Yellowstone Trivia: Including Crossword Puzzles, Quote Quests, Word Games & More.* Helena, MT: Riverbend Publishing, 2006.

Yellowstone Resources & Issues 2005. Division of Interpretation, Yellowstone National Park, 2005.

CAPTURED BY INDIANS

"Battle of the Big Hole." *Wikipedia.* https://en.wikipedia.org/ wiki/Battle_of_the_Big_Hole.

Clawson, Calvin C., and Eugene Lee Silliman. *A Ride to the Infernal Regions: Yellowstone's First Tourists.* Helena, MT: Riverbend Publishing, 2003.

Haines, Aubrey L. *The Yellowstone Story: A History of Our First National Park*. Yellowstone Association for Natural Science, History & Education, 1996.

"Nez Perce War." *Wikipedia*. https://en.wikipedia.org/wiki/Nez_Perce_War.

Schweber, Nate. *Fly Fishing Yellowstone National Park: An Insider's Guide to the 50 Best Places*. Mechanicsburg, PA: Stackpole/Headwater Books, 2012.

Watry, Elizabeth A. "Emma Carpenter Cowan." In *Women in Wonderland: Lives, Legends and Legacies of Yellowstone National Park*, 5–21. Helena, MT: Riverbend Publishing, 2012.

NATURE'S LAUNDROMAT

Chittenden, Hiram Martin. *The Yellowstone National Park: Historical and Descriptive*. London: Forgotten Books, 2016.

Clawson, Calvin C., and Eugene Lee Silliman. *A Ride to the Infernal Regions: Yellowstone's First Tourists*. Helena, MT: Riverbend Publishing, 2003.

Grundhauser, Eric. "The Embarrassing History of Crap Thrown into Yellowstone's Geysers." *Atlas Obscura*, April 13, 2017. www.atlasobscura.com/articles/yellowstone-geysers-trash-garbage.

Miller, M. Mark. "Angering Old Faithful in Yellowstone Park with a Load of Dirty Laundry in 1877." *Yellowstone Gate*, October 10, 2012. www.yellowstonegate.com/2012/10/angering-old-faithful-yellowstone-park-load-of-dirty-laundry-1877/.

"Queen's Laundry Bath House." *Wikipedia*. https://en.wikipedia
.org/wiki/Queen%27s_Laundry_Bath_House.

Reichard, Sean. "Yellowstone History: Queen's Laundry."
Yellowstone Insider, October 17, 2016. https://yellowstone
insider.com/2016/10/17/yellowstone-history-queens-laundry/.

"Things Stuffed Down Yellowstone's Geysers." *My Yellowstone
Park*, March 3, 2014. www.yellowstonepark.com/things-to-do/
yellowstone-geyser-damage.

Winser, Henry J. "The Lower Geyser Basin." In *The Yellowstone
National Park: A Manual for Tourists: Being a Description of
the Mammoth Hot Springs, the Geyser Basins, the Cataracts, the
Cañons, and Other Features of the Land of Wonders*, 37–40.
New York: Putnam, 1883.

YANCEY'S GHOST

Beal, Merrill D. "Uncle John Yancey." In *The Story of Man in
Yellowstone*, 203–5. Ann Arbor: University of Michigan Press,
1992.

Chittenden, Hiram Martin. *The Yellowstone National Park:
Historical and Descriptive*. London: Forgotten Books, 2016.

Clawson, Calvin C., and Eugene Lee Silliman. *A Ride to the
Infernal Regions: Yellowstone's First Tourists*. Helena, MT:
Riverbend Publishing, 2003.

"Ghosts of Yellowstone." *My Yellowstone Park*, October 31, 2013.
www.yellowstonepark.com/park/ghosts-of-yellowstone.

Goss, Robert V. "Roosevelt & Yancey's." In *Geyser Bob's Yellowstone Park Historical Service*, 2009. http://geyserbob.org/hot-roosevelt .html.

Schlosser, S. E. "Yancey's Ghost." In *Spooky Yellowstone: Tales of Hauntings, Strange Happenings, and Other Local Lore*, 112–18. Guilford, CT: Globe Pequot Press, 2013.

SHIPWRECK ON YELLOWSTONE LAKE

Freeman, Gary. "Wyoming's Demise of the 'E. C. Waters' Boat in Yellowstone Park." KGAB, February 2, 2017. http://kgab.com/ wyomings-demise-of-the-e-c-waters-in-yellowstone-national -park/.

Stark, Mike. "E. C. Waters Left to Rot in Yellowstone National Park." *Billings Gazette*, July 17, 2007. http://billingsgazette .com/news/state-and-regional/wyoming/e-c-waters-left-to-rot -in-yellowstone-national-park/article_1e5b84e8-8cf4-5505 -857b-bfdd9cfe070b.html.

Stark, Mike. *Wrecked in Yellowstone: Greed, Obsession, and the Untold Story of Yellowstone's Most Infamous Shipwreck.* Helena, MT: Riverbend Publishing, 2016.

OBSIDIAN CLIFF

Alexander, Thomas. "Paleo-Indians." Utah Department of Heritage & Arts, Utah Division of State History, August 16, 2016. https://heritage.utah.gov/tag/obsidian.

"Beringia." *Wikipedia.* https://en.wikipedia.org/wiki/Beringia.

Chittenden, Hiram Martin. *The Yellowstone National Park: Historical and Descriptive*. London: Forgotten Books, 2016.

"Exploring the Uses of Rocks in Indian Culture." Rock Cycle, Math/Science Nucleus. www.msnucleus.org/membership/html/k-6/rc/rocks/4/rcr4_3a.html.

Haines, Aubrey L. *The Yellowstone Story: A History of Our First National Park*. Yellowstone Association for Natural Science, History & Education, 1996.

Knight, Jason. "Making Arrowheads: The Ancient Art of Flint Knapping." Alderleaf Wilderness College. www.wilderness college.com/making-arrowheads.html.

"Obsidian." *Wikipedia*. https://en.wikipedia.org/wiki/Obsidian.

"Obsidian Cliff." Yellowstone National Park, National Park Service, U.S. Department of the Interior. www.nps.gov/yell/learn/historyculture/obsidiancliff.htm.

Vestal, Stanley. *Jim Bridger, Mountain Man: A Biography*. Lincoln: University of Nebraska Press, 1970.

INDEX

ABOUT THE AUTHOR

When five-year-old **Ednor Therriault** caught his first trout on a fly rod at Nevada Creek Dam near Helmville, Montana, he hadn't a clue that he himself would one day become hooked on the history of the fascinating and beautiful land that surrounded him. In his 2009 book *Montana Curiosities* for Globe Pequot Press, Ednor explored the Big Sky State from Alzada to the Yaak, chronicling the oddball places, people, and events that contribute to Montana's colorful character. The book became the top seller in Globe Pequot's Curiosities series, and the second edition was released in 2016.

Ednor's writing can be seen in the *Missoula Independent*, *Mountain Outlaw* magazine, *Montana Magazine*, and other regional publications. He is currently seeking a publisher for his first novel, *Stealing Motown*.

Ednor is also a musician, working under the *nom de guerre* Bob Wire. He's released five albums of original music, and his band was twice voted the best in Missoula. In 2007 Bob Wire was named Missoula's Entertainer of the Year.

Currently living and working in Missoula, Ednor is always on the lookout for the quirkier facets of Western lifestyle and history that dance around the edges of the well known. He and his wife, Shannon, are frequent visitors to Yellowstone National Park and have celebrated a few anniversaries there, drinking champagne toasts by the light of a campfire.